# The Historic Chicago Greystone:

A User's Guide for Renovating and Maintaining Your Home

*Edited by Dan Wheeler, FAIA, James Wheaton, and Tasneem A. Chowdhury*

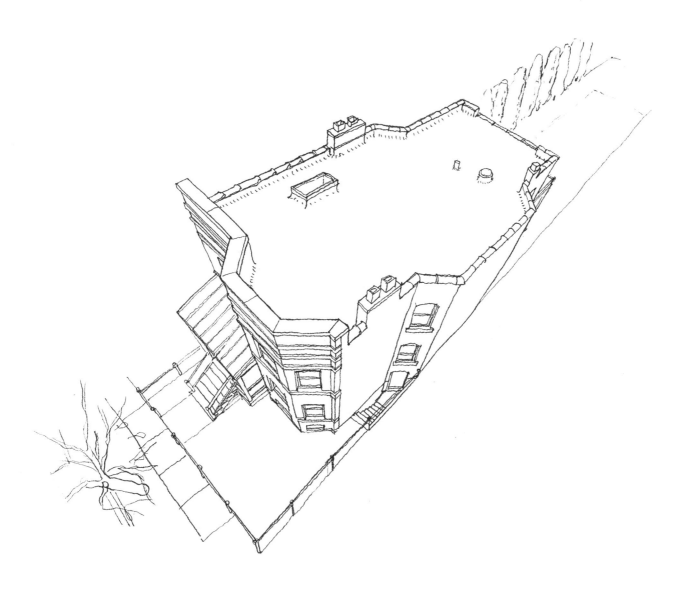

# Preface

The Westside neighborhood of North Lawndale and the City of Chicago offers a unique opportunity to examine some principles of community development. With almost 2000 limestone-clad buildings, or Greystones, North Lawndale is at the center of the City's "Greystone belt." How can a building type serve as a model for revitalizing a community? How can a sense of "pride-in-place" contribute to a movement that will foster re-investment in an aging housing stock? And how can Chicago learn from this experiment and tweak it for other communities that also hold large numbers of Greystones, communities that might have significantly different needs than North Lawndale. I believe that the questions raised above can be answered, and that Chicago can have a community development model that resonates around the country. Gerald and Lorean Earles, Cook County Commissioner Robert Steele, Alderman Sharon Denise Dixon, Annie Lott, Doretha Penn, Tracy and Sherry Scott, Cedric and Nicole Cabell-Pope are some of the many community residents and Greystone owners who believe so too. They have challenged us to think about the importance of these 100+ year old buildings, to craft solutions and examples for restoring them, for making them more livable, for using them to enhance a shared sense of community, and, indeed, for "greening" the Greystone. This broad and diverse group of community residents, coupled with preservationists, public officials, foundations, architects and planners, and other partners, including the "New Communities" leadership have been assembled to assist in this effort. They participated in focus groups, community meetings, charrettes, and many late night conversations. One result of this effort is this volume, *The Historic Chicago Greystone: A User's Guide for Renovating and Maintaining Your Home.*

Edited by Dan Wheeler of the School of Architecture at the University of Illinois at Chicago and Wheeler Kearns Architects, James K. (Jim) Wheaton, Deputy Director of Neighborhood Housing Services of Chicago, and Tasneem A. Chowdhury of the School of Architecture, University of Illinois at Chicago, this volume shows the possibilities of restoring, revitalizing, and remaking these century old buildings. Robert Bruegmann lets us know that the Greystone is "no ordinary building," and should be "celebrated as one of the great architectural achievements of all time." Roberta Feldman and Deirdre Colgan demonstrate the consummate vitality and innovativeness of the building by literally "moving the walls." Tom Forman and Rachel Forman give us a primer on the building — there is a difference between Indiana limestone and Joliet limestone. David Brown and Tasneem A. Chowdhury help us keep our language straight so that we might all speak the language of parapet walls and beadboard ceilings. Darris Shaw and Matt Cole help us think through the process of selecting contractors, as well as providing technical assistance through Neighborhood Housing Services of Chicago that can allow many owners to safely, economically, and efficiently manage their Greystone rehabilitation projects.

Dan Wheeler's effort deserves special notice. To pull this work — *The Historic Chicago Greystone: A User's Guide for Renovating and Maintaining Your Home* — together, Dan really did do as Roberta Feldman pointed out in her section... he literally "moved the walls" of the Greystone at 1841 S. Spaulding Avenue in an effort to help prove Bob Bruegmann's point that these are "no ordinary buildings." Dan also figured out before the rest of the group that 1841 S. Spaulding was indeed clad in Tom Forman's Indiana limestone. As the façade of the building had been previously painted, none of us could see the luster of the limestone underneath the "gunboat grey" paint. Dan clearly could. His sharp eyes and steady hands are evident in the beautiful hand-drawn illustrations documenting the different processes of restoring the Spaulding house.

Tasneem A. Chowdhury's efforts are also noted. Tasneem has been the indispensable point person in bringing this work to fruition. She constantly kept everyone thinking about deadlines, and about being creative... two concepts she pointed out that are not necessarily mutually exclusive. We all benefited from her insights.

I must also mention the generous contribution of the Richard H. Driehaus Foundation. Richard Driehaus and the Foundation's Executive Director, Sunny Fischer, have been exemplars and stewards of Chicago's architectural and cultural gems. They have recognized and supported the effort undertaken by Neighborhood Housing Services of Chicago, community residents, and all the other partners and friends to celebrate what has often been thought of as just an ordinary Chicago building type. Richard and Sunny clearly agree that the Chicago Greystone is no ordinary building.

These groups, and all the other contributors, have created a book complementing the earlier volume — *The Chicago Greystone in Historic North Lawndale* — that helped launch the Historic Chicago Greystone Initiative®. Together, these two volumes frame the Chicago Greystone in its historical context; place it at the center of the city's urban fabric and development as the city grows west, north, and south from its downtown core; show the wave of ethnic and racial groups relying upon this housing type as a base for settling into the new and burgeoning Chicago; how the building type can serve as a compelling community revitalization strategy that can build pride in aging communities; and ultimately, as an incredibly beautiful icon for communities and all of Chicago. A notable achievement, indeed...

*Charles Leeks*
*Neighborhood Director*
*Neighborhood Housing Services of Chicago*
*North Lawndale Office*

4  **City of Chicago**
**Richard M. Daley, Mayor**

**Department of Environment**

Sadhu A. Johnston
Commissioner

Twenty-fifth Floor
30 North LaSalle Street
Chicago, Illinois 60602-2575
(312) 744-7606 (Voice)
(312) 744-6451 (FAX)
(312) 744-3586 (TTY)

http://www.cityofchicago.org

July 6, 2007

Historic Chicago Greystone Initiative
c/o Neighborhood Housing Services of Chicago, Inc.
1279 North Milwaukee Avenue, 5th Floor
Chicago, Illinois 60622

The City of Chicago Department of Environment is proud to participate in the Historic Chicago Greystone Initiative launched by Neighborhood Housing Services of Chicago. As a collaborative of concerned stakeholders including citizens, non-profits, businesses, academic institutions, and local government, the Greystone Initiative and supporting Greystone Guidebooks demonstrate Mayor Daley's commitment to implementing environmental innovations and strategies that are beneficial for the health of citizens and communities. We especially commend the Greystone Initiative's goal of promoting energy conservation and the use of "green" technology in the renovation of historic buildings.

The Department of Environment is proud to join the North Lawndale community in the implementation of the Greystone Initiative. As an active member of the Steering Team and Greystone Guidebook Committee, the Department participated in the development of a strategic plan for the Initiative, and provided technical support on issues pertaining to energy conservation and "green" building technologies. This Guidebook is a significant achievement and an invaluable aid to Greystone owners in renovating and preserving the architectural integrity of their homes. It will encourage Greystone owners to be proactive in restoring buildings, preserve the historic character of the neighborhood, and identify new opportunities to incorporate environmentally sustainable and energy efficient components into the renovation process.

North Lawndale's cultural and physical heritage, including its magnificent Greystones, is one of Chicago's most treasured assets. We are proud to support the North Lawndale community in their efforts to restore and revitalize their neighborhood's unique heritage.

Sincerely,

Sadhu A. Johnston
Commissioner
Department of Environment

# NEIGHBORHOOD HOUSING SERVICES OF CHICAGO, INC.

*Rebuilding Chicago's Neighborhoods*

1279 N. Milwaukee Ave., 5th Floor
Chicago, Illinois 60622
773 329-4010
fax: 773-329-4120
www.nhschicago.org

September, 2007

In June 2006, Neighborhood Housing Services of Chicago, Inc. (NHS), its partners, and local residents launched the Historic Chicago Greystone Initiative® in front of a recently rehabbed greystone two flat in North Lawndale. Attendees had the opportunity to tour the building and see first hand the potential embodied in the renovation these historic properties – from the glinting limestone facade, carefully cleaned of years of paint, to the reconfigured living spaces re-designed to better meet the needs of a contemporary homeowner.

In the more than one year since that warm summer day, I am happy to report that public response to the Historic Chicago Greystone Initiative® has been strong and growing. Some Greystone owners are seeking guidance and resources to address particular building issues. How, for example, can they appropriately restore their property's limestone façade or what can they do to help keep their basement dry? Others are seeking solutions to more comprehensive problems. How, for example, can they completely reconfigure the interior of their Greystone to better meet their family's needs?

The Guidebook you hold in your hand is meant to be an important first resource for those seeking to address these issues. It contains information relevant to a broad range of homeowners, from those trying to understand the basic maintenance needs of their Greystone to those interested in undertaking a complete "gut" rehab project. Developed in collaboration with architecture faculty from the University of Illinois at Chicago, it is based on lessons learned during the renovation of a "model greystone" in North Lawndale – a small, humble two-flat located just a stone's throw from where the Initiative was first launched.

Neighborhoods are fundamentally about the dynamic relationship between people, buildings and a given place. Families move in and move out; buildings get fixed; new homes are built; businesses open and close; and the people who live in the neighborhood get involved in block clubs and community groups, get to know their neighbors, raise their children, and put down their own roots. Across Chicago Greystone homes have played an important role in this process for more than 100 years. The Historic Chicago Greystone Initiative® – and this Guidebook – represents an important step in continuing this process long into the future.

Sincerely,

Bruce A. Gottschall
Executive Director
Neighborhood Housing Services of Chicago, Inc.

CHARTERED MEMBER

# Contents

# The Greystone:

## No Ordinary Building

This is a book about the Chicago Greystone. Most residents of the city are familiar with these limestone-fronted brick two-flat and three-flat buildings. They take them for granted as a characteristic part of the cityscape, as common and unremarkable as the workers' cottages and row houses that were put up in such quantities in the last two decades of the nineteenth century, or the bungalows and their two-flat and three-flat cousins that went up by the block in the 1920s.

For this reason it is not surprising that so few buildings of this type show up in the standard architectural histories of Chicago. The only Greystones illustrated in the best-known architectural guidebooks, the AIA Guide to Chicago and Chicago's Famous Buildings are single-family mansions. The workers' cottages and bungalows and their two- and three-unit cousins don't fare much better. They simply didn't count as important architecture for generations of architectural historians.

And yet, to overlook any of these buildings is to ignore what was and what remains one of the dominant housing types in the city of Chicago. For well over 50 years they have housed the majority of Chicago's families, serving generations of families who have been happy to call them home. Even today, despite age and decline, the workers' cottages, Greystones and bungalows that remain form the backbone of many of Chicago's neighborhoods. They ring the city center in three thick concentric bands, extending from close to the Loop at the center all the way, in many places, to the city limits.

Fortunately, by the early 21st century, with many neighborhoods showing ample signs of new life, there has been a new appreciation of these building types. In part this has been due to the continuing vitality of the preservation movement. Although this movement was long associated with efforts to save structures built by rich and famous individuals or designed by famous architects, since the 1960s it has increasingly come to be focused on the conservation of ensembles and the buildings that give even ordinary neighborhoods their distinctive texture and quality.

With this expanded preservation movement has come a corresponding grass-roots attempt to document and celebrate ordinary buildings as well as extraordinary ones because it has become clear that a city is not a collection of famous single buildings. In fact, what is arguably the greatest achievement of any city is not the single masterpieces but the way that thousands of builders, owners and architects managed to create, over the space of only a few decades, a coherent, useful fabric that has housed hundreds of thousands of Chicagoans ever since. This ought to be celebrated as one of the great architectural achievements of all time. Certainly there is nothing ordinary about the "ordinary" Greystone.

In plan the typical Greystone two- or three-flat was nothing more than a set of two or three workers' cottages, somewhat expanded in size and piled one on top of the other to form a multi-story building. This simple brick box, with a limestone façade to give it more dignity and presence along the street, was constructed by the thousands between the 1893 Chicago World's Fair and World War I. Each Greystone provided several families, often of very modest income, with accommodations that were much larger and better-equipped than anything they had been able to afford before.

For the renters, Greystones provided clean, sanitary apartments large enough in which to raise a family. The owners of the buildings often found financial security and upward economic mobility as rental income helped defray their own costs and as real estate appreciation over the years increased their net worth. The Greystone was one of the key machines in the transformation of working class Chicagoans into members of an expanding middle class.

The Greystones tend to cluster tightly along the great Park and Boulevard system laid out around the city in the late 19th century, linking Jackson and Washington Parks in the south to Logan Square and Lincoln Park in the north. Greystones stand in some of the city's most humble, as well as its most expensive neighborhoods. But in every neighborhood, the ordinary Greystone, with its carved ornament in Romanesque or classical style, whether expensively restored in an intact row in Lincoln Park or standing isolated and in need of repair on a block in North Lawndale, has a dignity and presence that commands respect.

The Chicago Greystone should not and cannot be considered in a vacuum. It was closely related to the standard building types that came before and after it in Chicago and was related to similar building types throughout urban America. The Greystone two- or three-flat is obviously related to the triple-decker in Boston and similar buildings throughout New England, with some important differences. The triple-decker was usually of frame construction and with its blunt, boxy proportions was clearly a multi-family building. One of the interesting things about the Chicago Greystone is that because it was constructed on standard size city lots with detailing that closely approximated the detailing found on single-family homes, there was no visual break between single-family homes and multi-family Greystones in most Chicago neighborhoods.

There are related building types, either in masonry or frame construction, found in all of the older cities of the Midwest and as far west as San Francisco. Everywhere they have been built, however, they defer to local traditions. In San Francisco, for example, the three-story three-unit frame structures constructed in the early twentieth century are obviously related to the frame row houses of the mid- and late Victorian era, so much so that these Edwardian boxes, which were probably painted white with delicately tinted ornament when first built, are today often given the robust paint schemes more appropriate to mid-19th century "painted ladies."

Fortunately, this confusion and ignorance about even the most basic facts concerning the average, ordinary fabric of our cities is starting to lift now that so many scholars, preservationists and ordinary citizens are focusing their attention on buildings like the two-flat or three-flat Greystone or any of the other basic building blocks of the 19th and early 20th century city. One of the great projects of the next decades for historians of architecture, government agencies and community groups will be to inventory America's basic building stock and try to write its history, not just in one place but in all its kaleidoscopic permutations across the continent.

The Historic Chicago Greystone Initiative® is a welcome sign that Chicagoans are rediscovering a key building type in their own back yard. Following the model of the Historic Chicago Bungalow Initiative, the Historic Chicago Greystone Initiative® seeks to celebrate and preserve this remarkable architectural legacy. Too many of these buildings disappeared during the difficult decades after World War II as great factories closed down and business and residents abandoned the city for the suburbs, but the wave of revitalization that is moving through older urban neighborhoods offers an opportunity to reverse that trend.

The Historic Chicago Greystone Initiative®, which debuted in the North Lawndale community in summer 2006, is a sign that Chicagoans have realized that it is time to protect, preserve and celebrate the Greystones that remain. These are sturdy buildings that, with some care and attention, are fully capable of serving for a second century as safe and comfortable housing, as well as a dignified and graceful backdrop to renewed communities and a resurgent city. This book is an attempt to guide Chicagoans in that process.

# A Case Study:

The Story of One Greystone

This story begins with an encounter with one such Greystone. Built as a two-flat nearly a hundred years ago, over the years it had been subjected to incremental modifications and repairs (or not), that ultimately rendered it uninhabitable and vacant. The University of Illinois' City Design Center and School of Architecture, along with Neighborhood Housing Services of Chicago took this building under their wing, and used it as a case study for this guidebook. While each Greystone has its own specific story, the story of this Greystone may inspire other resurrections.

While the building was vacant, the Greystone façade painted, the front porch long lost, the site overgrown — the house was found to be structurally sound. The existing basement was tall and fairly dry; the support posts charmingly made of tree trunks. The two floors, each separate dwelling units, were more or less in their original configurations, with a public room in front, bedrooms along the sides and a kitchen and bath toward the rear. A back porch, while appearing in reasonable condition, was found to be non-code compliant. To better understand the assignment, the team looked to what incremental work would be required to breathe new life into this Greystone. But first, let's step back, and understand what a Greystone is, and what its basics are ...

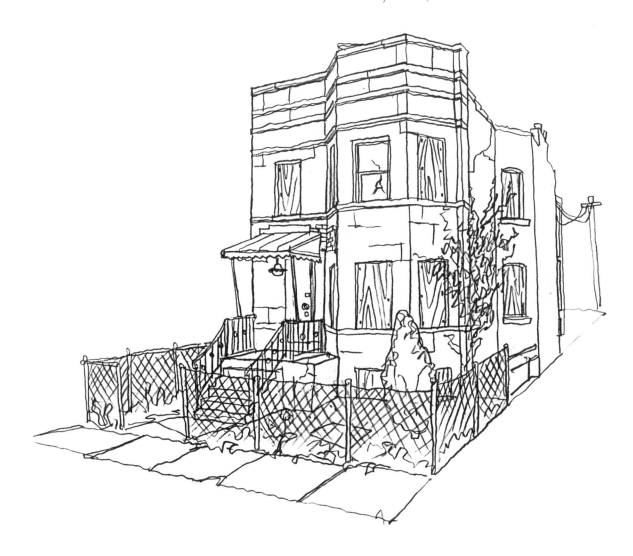

## Existing, unimproved condition

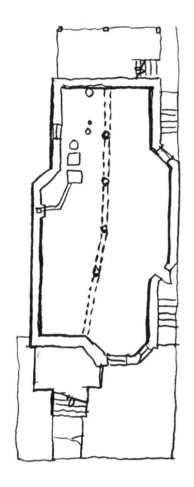

Basement

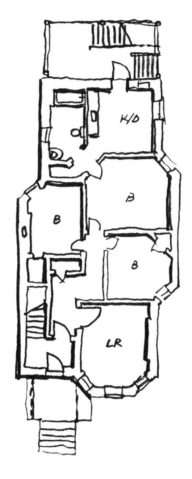

First Floor

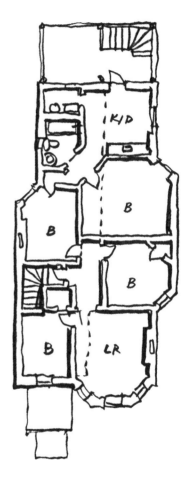

Second Floor

# Investigating Your Greystone

# Greystone Structure:
How It Stands Up

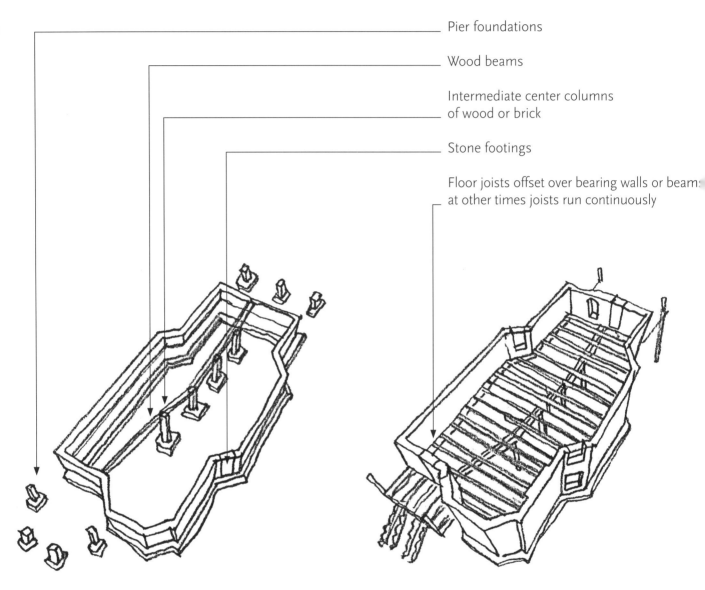

Pier foundations

Wood beams

Intermediate center columns
of wood or brick

Stone footings

Floor joists offset over bearing walls or beams
at other times joists run continuously

### The Foundation
Typically stone and brick perimeter, often set to sit
just above the level of ground water. Interior wood
posts support wood beams that carry the floor
structure above; porch structures are supported
by pier foundations; front stoops are constructed
of stone.

### Floor Framing
Inside the masonry walls, floor framing is wood.
At times the wood joists span from wall to wall
and are supported from below; at other times the
joists are discontinuous and bear on the beam/
wall below.

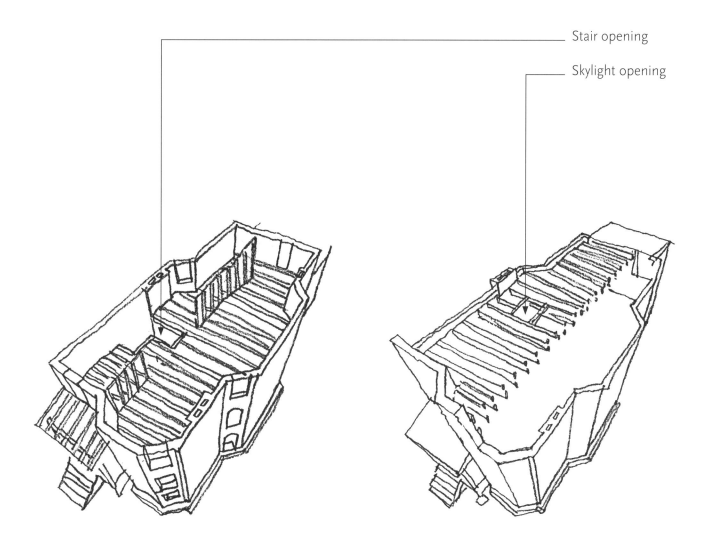

Stair opening

Skylight opening

## Interior Framing

Interior bearing walls typically run parallel to the exterior walls, aligning generally with the walls and beams below.

## Roof Framing

The roof slopes to the rear and the ceiling framing runs flat. The framing joists typically span from wall to wall, and are designed for supporting minimal loads, not for roof loads.

# Greystone Structure:

How It Stands Up *continued*

Gutter

Roof flashing

Roofing over roof sheathing

Porch column

Catch basin

Basement slabs were often unreinforced
concrete, 2 inch to 4 inch thick over sand
with no vapor barrier

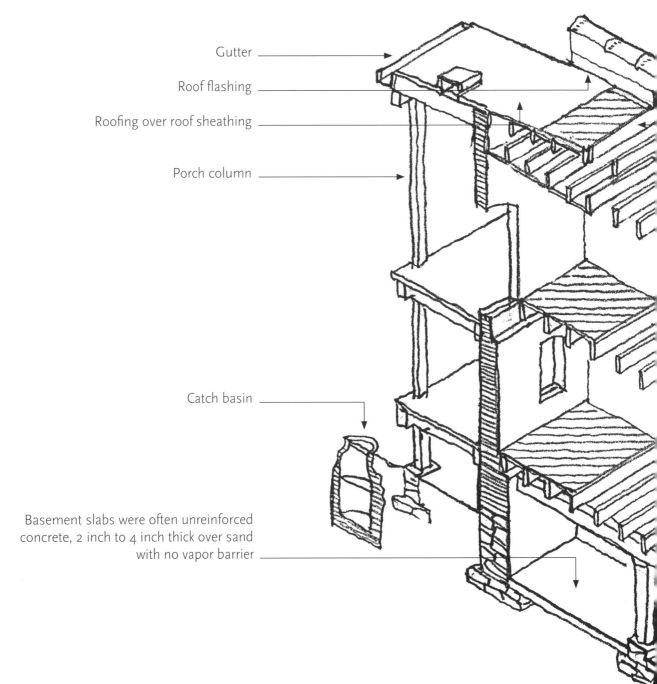

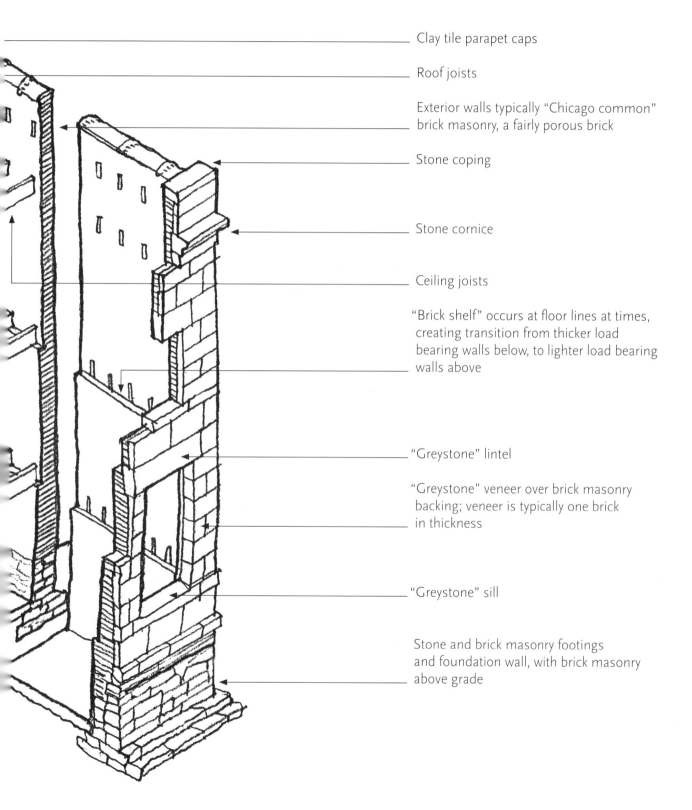

Clay tile parapet caps

Roof joists

Exterior walls typically "Chicago common" brick masonry, a fairly porous brick

Stone coping

Stone cornice

Ceiling joists

"Brick shelf" occurs at floor lines at times, creating transition from thicker load bearing walls below, to lighter load bearing walls above

"Greystone" lintel

"Greystone" veneer over brick masonry backing; veneer is typically one brick in thickness

"Greystone" sill

Stone and brick masonry footings and foundation wall, with brick masonry above grade

# Basic Systems:
Mechanical, Electrical and Plumbing

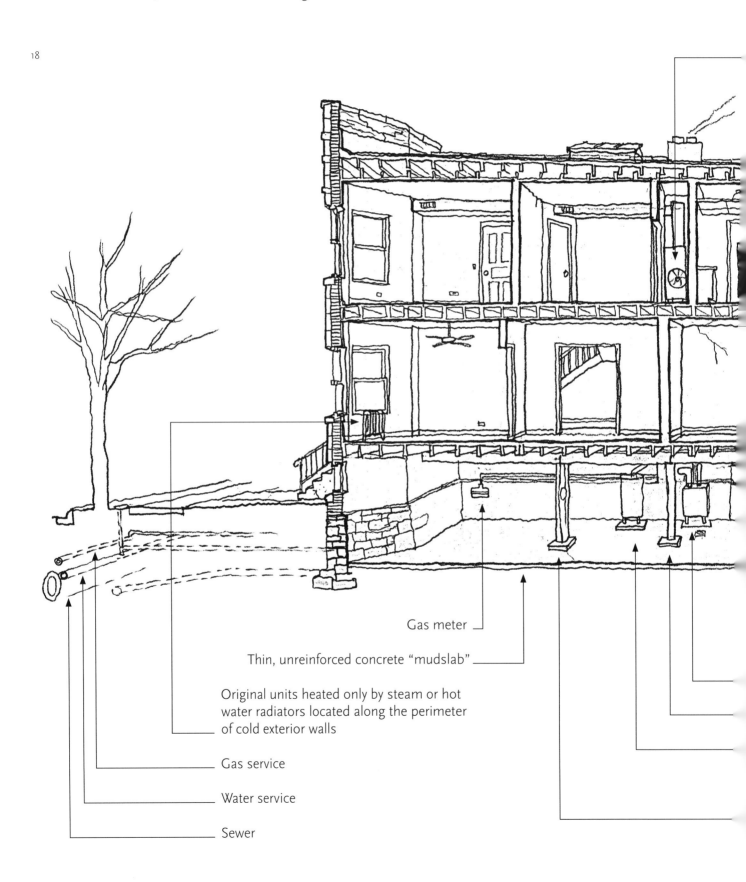

Gas meter

Thin, unreinforced concrete "mudslab"

Original units heated only by steam or hot
water radiators located along the perimeter
of cold exterior walls

Gas service

Water service

Sewer

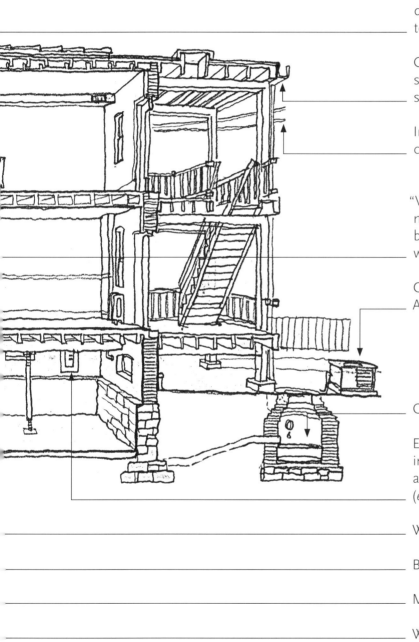

"Modernized" dwellings at times are heated and cooled by "air handling units" (A.H.U.s) using air pushed from a fan unit through ducts to the building's perimeters, and returned through grills to a centrally located unit

Bath, kitchen "vent-stack" that vents odors from a "waste stack;" a "waste stack" directs kitchen and sanitary waste directly to the sewer

Gutter collects rain, directs it to downspout to catch basin and then to storm/ sanitary sewer

Incoming, overhead telephone, electric cable services — typically from rear alley

"Wet wall" describes an area where the primary plumbing "stack" is located; typically baths and kitchens share a common wet wall, but not always

Often exposed, noisy condensing unit (for AC) in forced air systems

Catch basin (for storm water)

Electrical panel, one per unit; occasionally in multi-unit buildings, there is an additional one for "common areas" (*e.g.*, rear, porch, stairwell)

Water service valve

Boiler (for radiators)

Masonry flue

Water heater

Various forms of support columns will be encountered (*e.g.*, wood tree trunks, posts, brick piers, steel)

# Interior Detailing:
Original Practices

**Original Interior Construction**

Original trim allowed for material movement and construction tolerance, relying on multiple pieces of wood trim to ease transitions of imperfect hand construction.

Window opening: note that interior brick is set back to allow for weight box of window

Wood double-hung window: note side (jamb) weight box that houses counter balancing metal weights

Wood storm window

Window sill (stool)

Window apron

Door/window "casing"

Plaster mixed with horse hair over wood lath attached to wood strips set in brick courses

"Plinth block"

"3 piece base" trim including cap, standing base, and base shoe, the latter often removable to refinish floors

"Cementitious parging" to help retard water penetration; brick and stone foundations

Paneled door (stile and rail)

"Saddle" threshold between rooms at door allowed for material, thickness changes

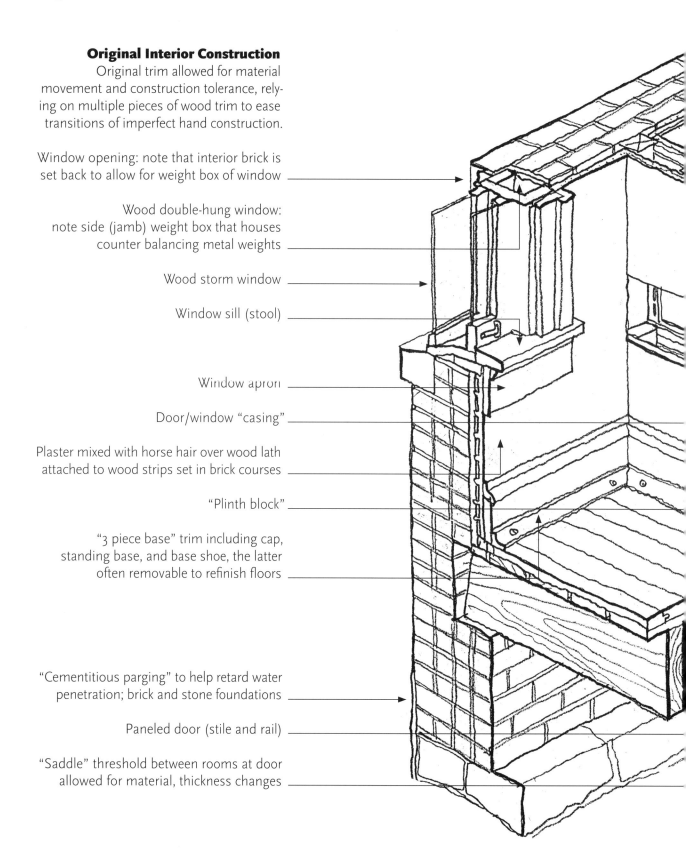

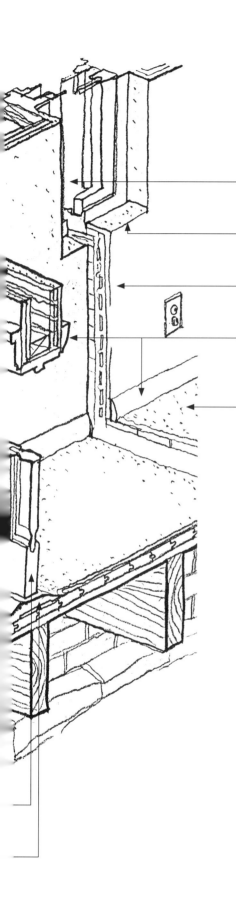

## "Modernization"

Often the existing original trim has been removed and covered over with new finishes, rather than having received more substantial renovations.

Aluminum storm windows over existing single pane windows

Drywall is laminated over existing plaster and "returned" to window, eliminating wood around windows

Exterior walls of brick plaster and drywall provide limited, if any, insulating value

One piece "ranch molding" is often found at baseboards and around doorways, as a way to reduce material and labor

Carpet/pad often cover existing patched floors

# Greystone "Outback"

Parapets exposed to elements
and freeze/thaw; may require
tuck-pointing or rebuilding

Gutters often fill with debris, need
yearly maintenance

Existing porches, while in apparent sound
repair, may not comply with current
codes for construction; floor loadings
criteria (maximum supported weight) are
critical to safety, as are railing heights
and requirements to prevent climbing

Overhead electric, telephone, and, at times,
cable services may impact tree placement

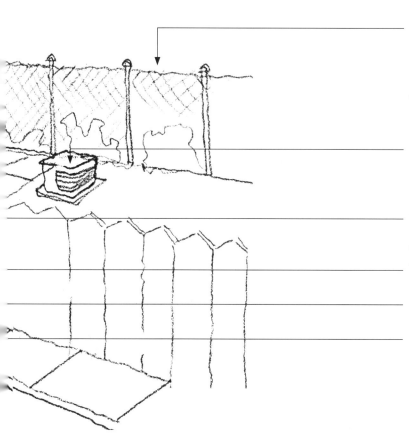

Often uncoordinated fencing in poor
repair; verify upon which property it lies
from the plat of survey

Air conditioning condensing units,
often located in the rear yard, impact
use of space by their size and the
sound they generate

Catch basins collect storm water from
roof, and need inspection and cleanout
from time to time

Concrete paving heaved, sloping
toward house

Boarded up windows, doors

Ivy degrading brick masonry

# Assessing Your Greystone

**What do you have? A quick assessment, step by step...**

**Building Occupancy** *(current or planned)*
- three- or four-flat
- two-flat
- single family
- check local codes for legality of residential units in basements

**Intangibles** *(assist in setting value)*
- location (transit, schools, shopping)
- views toward: "curb appeal"
- views outward: "dwelling appeal"
- solar orientation (impact on heating/cooling)
- adjacent structures
- drainage patterns

**Relative Conditions** *(a sampling of concerns, often reviewed with assistance of home inspector, architect or contractor)*
- structural condition
- age, condition of roof
- age, condition of "shell" (stone, masonry, windows, doors)
- porch, stair code compliance
- age, condition of systems (electrical, plumbing, mechanical)
- evidence of water damage
- evidence of asbestos, lead-based paint
- condition of bath/kitchens
- conditions of interior finishes
- condition/definition of landscape

**Weigh the building condition and anticipated function with local codes, available funding, and schedule, to help determine next steps: what you can do, and what may lie ahead.**

**Maintainer**
*$, Hours or Days*
Carefully selected improvements to building and grounds to sustain a sound, weather-tight building shell. Generally no permit required.

**Fixer-upper**
*$$, Days or Weeks*
A la carte improvements to upgrade stable properties. These improvements are generally considered "cosmetic" and require few (repair) permits.

**Rehabber**
*$$$, Weeks or Months*
Conversions in buildings beyond cosmetic improvements, to replace systems beyond repair, to make moderate improvements to the basic configuration and to better optimize the use of the property. Often will require "repair permits" or general permits when involving multiple systems/trades or dealing with structural changes.

**Total Gut**
*$$$$, Months or Years*
Conversion of a building with stable shell with little value in its existing condition. Uses an existing shell to support a new configuration of living, drawing upon the best in current planning and construction practices. General construction permits will be required.

# Assessing Your Greystone

| | Maintainer | Fixer-upper |
|---|---|---|
| **Health and Life Safety Improvements** | · install and maintain heat/smoke/CO detectors<br>· install safety glass in doors, windows as required by code<br>· locate and seal exposed lead paint and asbestos materials<br>· inspect/repair stair railings<br>· inspect/repair porch structures<br>· inspect/maintain flues/chimneys | · clean catch basin<br>· rod out sewer lines<br>· rebuild/replace porch per code<br>· use Low or No VOC paints<br>· perform test for Radon<br>· perform a blower door test and comprehensive air sealing |
| **Energy, Sustainability Improvements** | · weather-strip windows, doors<br>· service existing mechanical equipment<br>· insulate exposed duct work<br>· insulate pre-1992 water heaters<br>· replace incandescent light bulbs with compact fluorescents | · install water saving fixtures<br>· install Energy Star® appliances<br>· install reflective roof coating onto existing roofing.<br>· install historically appropriate storm windows, doors<br>· install occupancy sensors<br>· install programmable thermostats |
| **Restoration and Renovation Improvements** | · replace broken glass<br>· strip, paint and repair windows<br>· inspect and repair roofing and flashings on primary and secondary roofs<br>· seal copings<br>· inspect/repair/maintain gutters and downspouts<br>· repair finishes<br>· seal open cracks at exterior walls/openings | · restore/replace kitchen and bathroom, using energy-efficient fixtures and appliances<br>· restore, replace interior finishes<br>· repair/replace poorly installed doors and windows<br>· insulate unused spaces (attic, crawl spaces)<br>· restore/replace porches<br>· tuck-point masonry<br>· pressure wash or chemically clean front façade |
| **Landscape Improvements** | · repair, paint fencing<br>· grade slope away from house<br>· remove ivy from masonry<br>· prune landscape, remove plantings from immediately adjacent to structure<br>· add hanging baskets or spring flowering bulbs<br>· contact 311 to request a new tree on the parkway | · repair paving<br>· install new planting<br>· add new fencing to better define, secure yards<br>· install ornamental gardens with flowering perennials and groundcover<br>· install rain barrels on downspouts |

| | Rehabber | Total Gut |
|---|---|---|
| **Health and Life Safety Improvements** | • remove ("abate") sources of lead paint, asbestos<br>• install interior sub-soil sump and sewage ejector to help prevent flooding, mold<br>• parge interior of masonry foundations to help control moisture/vapor drive into basement | • optimize quality of daylight and air quality in basic planning and system selection, (*i.e.* installing ERV fresh-air makeup systems for HVAC)<br>• reduce sound pollution via elimination of condensing units, use of highly insulated glass and insulation systems<br>• conceal, protect utility lines below grade.<br>• consider use of residential fire sprinkler system |
| **Energy, Sustainability Improvements** | • install high efficiency furnace, boiler, water heaters<br>• retrofit boiler controls and radiator controls<br>• install new mechanical system distribution<br>• perform comprehensive insulation (attic, sidewalls)<br>• upgrade windows to historically appropriate low-E models<br>• recycle construction and demolition waste | • excavate exterior perimeter and waterproof<br>• insulate basement walls<br>• install a geothermal heat system<br>• install solar panels to supplement electric use<br>• install solar thermal panels to supplement space heat, cooling and hot water usage<br>• consider use of floor slabs, water walls as "heat sinks"<br>• create a comprehensive recycling plan for all rehab waste |
| **Restoration and Renovation Improvements** | • install new roof, gutters<br>• install new electric, water services<br>• combine units, open rooms via structural changes to afford greater use and facilitate passage of light and air<br>• install new systems to new baths, kitchens<br>• upgrade doors to historically appropriate solid core, weather-stripped models<br>• use recycled content or sustainably harvested lumber | • level/replace floor structures<br>• consider new plan arrangements to optimize light and air, multi-functioning spaces<br>• consider incorporation of radiant heat<br>• install all new systems, finishes, fittings, in consideration of energy usage, ideally with high recycled content value. (*i.e.* flooring, carpet, cabinets, glass) |
| **Landscape Improvements** | • replace paving (with permeable systems)<br>• install larger flowering plants (trees or shrubs) to shade openings in summer months<br>• add a raised-bed vegetable garden and compost pile<br>• add a rain garden or rain barrel | • install new parkway sidewalk, trees (with city assistance)<br>• install underground elec./tel./cable service<br>• replace porch, deck or garage<br>• install low-flow "smart" irrigation system<br>• install a green roof on primary roof as well as potentially on accessory structures (garage) to optimize water retention<br>• consider interior/exterior mudrooms/greenhouses as airlocks/transitions into/out of residence |

# Maintainer

The Maintainer: An owner who can take on periodic improvements to a property with occasional assistance. This implies that the property is in relatively sound condition, with the chief activities being the maintenance of the exterior shell against the elements and protecting the occupants from hazardous conditions. Some examples include:

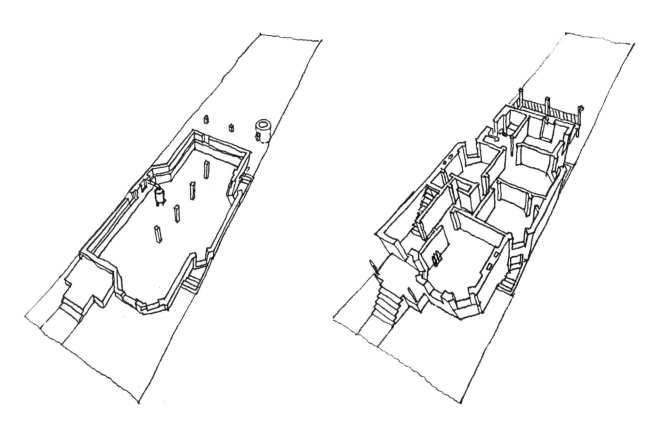

### Basement/Grounds

Maintain the condition of mechanical, electrical and plumbing services, including flues and chimneys. Install smoke and CO detectors in the basement. Keep wood from contact with dampness which can facilitate mold. Keep grades around house sloping away from building. Maintain floor drains.

### Interior

Maintain paint finishes so not to be friable. Install smoke and CO detectors as codes require. Replace light bulbs with energy-efficient fluorescent lamps which come "color corrected."

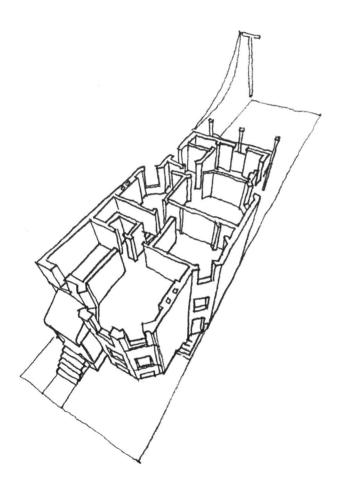

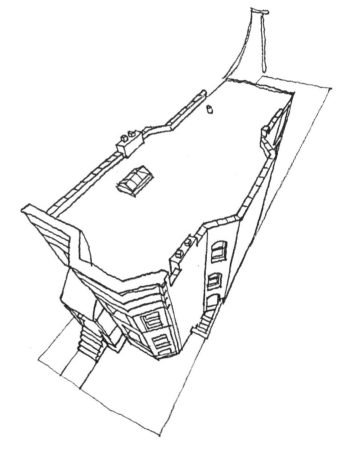

**Exterior Shell**

Maintain windows and doors, seal non-operable units and weatherstrip all operable units. Remove ivy on masonry and patch cracks in masonry. Have porches inspected for code compliance. Repair and maintain exterior trim, fencing, etc. by upkeeping finishes.

**Roof**

Clean gutter, inspect and patch roofing if required. Copings/parapet caps to be sealed with soft sealant to prevent water infiltration into masonry.

# Fixer-upper

The Fixer-upper: A small team of individuals working with an owner, take on specific upgrades to a property. Typically projects are cosmetic in nature, but on occasion result in more substantial changes or larger impact maintenance programs. Some examples include:

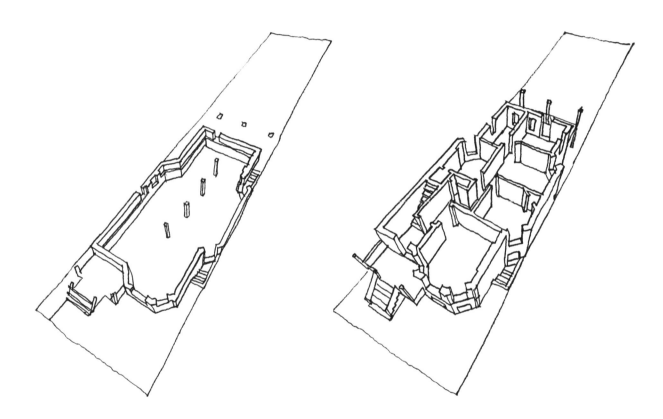

### Basement/Grounds

Clean out existing catch basin of sediment. Provide cementitious parging (coating) on exterior/interior basement walls. Rod out sewer lines often filled with tree roots.

### Interior

Upgrade baths and kitchens, using water-conserving plumbing fixtures and Energy Star®-label (energy-efficient) appliances. Install programmable thermostats and occupancy sensors as energy savers. Paint with Low VOC paint.

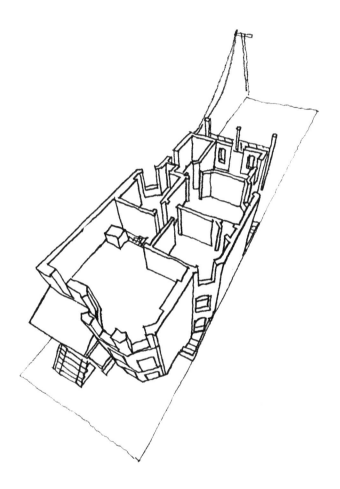

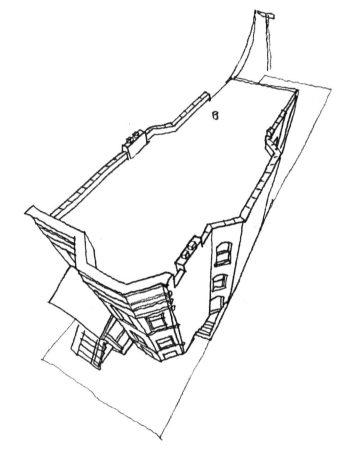

**Exterior Shell**

Inspect/rebuild porches that are beyond repair to meet building codes. Tuck-point masonry, pressure wash or chemically clean front façade stone. Do not sand-blast or use other abrasive cleaning methods due to risk of damaging Greystone.

**Roof**

Paint/coat roofing with reflective coating to minimize solar heat gain in summer.

# Rehabber

The Rehabber: An owner who chooses to pursue more extensive upgrades to the property, either for conversion or because existing conditions call for it. Often the primary systems of the property are replaced, along with strategic plan changes to optimize use to meet current needs.

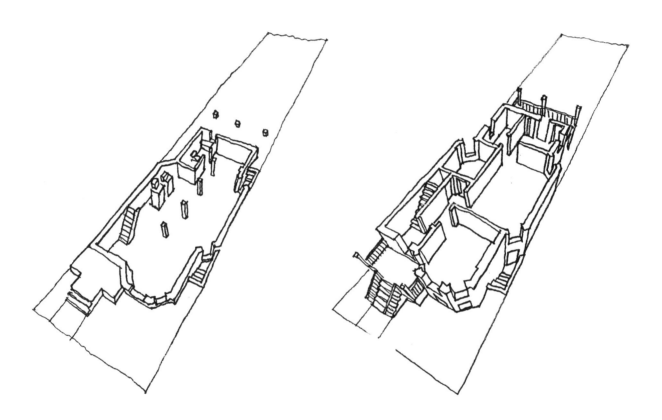

### Basement/Grounds

New mechanical, electrical and plumbing systems are installed, with a more formal build-out of the space for use by residents. Sump pit(s) are often installed to prevent flooding and to insure operation of basement plumbing systems.

### Interior

In conjunction with new mechanicals, specific walls are removed to facilitate new programmed spaces. Non-bearing walls are removed to provide greater openness. New flooring coincides with new spaces. *Note:* typically these improvements involve laminating finishes over existing surfaces rather than wholesale replacement.

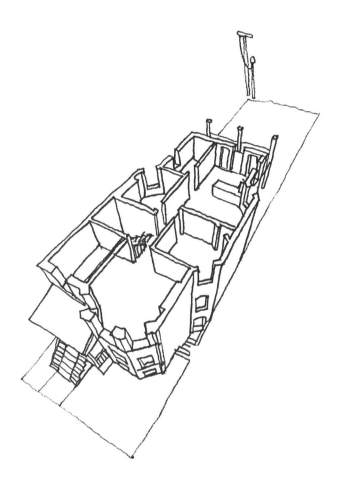

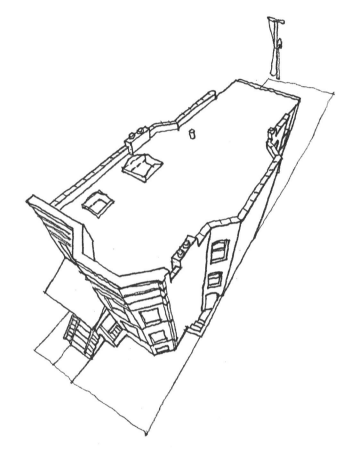

## Exterior Shell

Existing overhead electric services are often replaced with in-ground feeds for greater safety and to be visually more discreet. New windows and doors make for a more weather-tight and energy-efficient building. *Note:* historically appropriate windows and doors should be used to maintain building's original character.

## Roof

With greater investments occurring below, a new roof is highly recommended. Removal of existing roof allows for full inspection and rebuilding of "soft" parapet walls and roof sheathing, and allows for installation of new skylights, etc. Roof insulation is added to improve energy efficiency and reduce operating costs.

# Total Gut

The "total gut" owner enlists a larger team, involving architect/engineers, to completely rethink the possibilities of the structure, while working within the confines of the existing shell. While most demanding in time and cost, the property is often economical to purchase given its existing condition, and the potential is the greatest for improvement. While floor framing often is left in place, even this can be removed if required. Building permits are required.

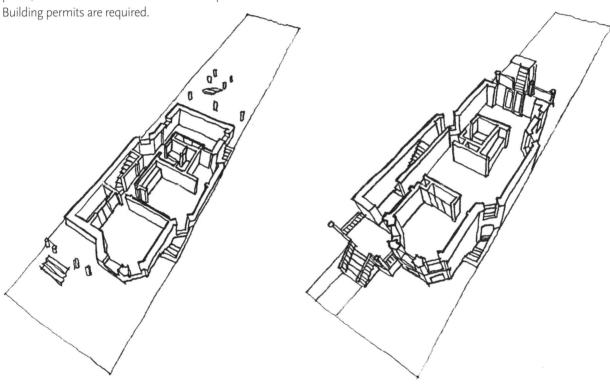

### Basement/Grounds

Typically the basement slab is removed and occasionally lowered, and the exterior face of foundation walls are waterproofed to allow the investment of a full build-out of the lower levels. Local codes regarding basement units must be observed.

### Interior

New unit configurations often dictate new plans. Once stairs/exiting paths are located, bath and kitchen cores are located. *Note*: while two exits are typically required per floor, these at times may be reduced. Consult the local building code.

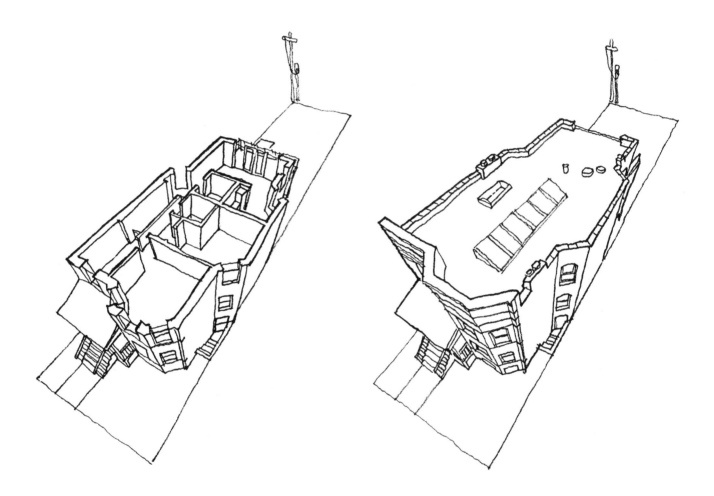

**Exterior Shell**

New porches provide opportunities to optimally restore the character and quality of the front façade, while the rear façade can be more appropriately adapted to the private rear yard.

**Roof**

The new roof corresponds with the new plan below, complete with skylight, vents, etc. New uses can be entertained, including use of exterior decks, "green" roof constructions, and/or use of photovoltaic panels or wind generators for energy production.

# Restoring/Renovating Your Greystone

Fig. 1b

# Moving the Walls:

## Variation on Plan Layouts

You own and live in a historic Chicago Greystone or are considering buying one. The historic Greystone is a design that is generally 100 years old, designed for families and lifestyles of that time. This arrangement works fine for some people, providing a large number of rooms in a small amount of space; and, if you're lucky, all or most of the original architectural details and cabinetry. *(See Fig. 1a–1c)*

Making some modest changes will provide for more natural light, better views of the rear garden, more closet space, or a modernized kitchen or bathroom. For other Greystone owners, more extensive changes may be necessary because the arrangement or size of the rooms may not fit their lifestyle requirements, or, if a multi-family building, the needs of renters. The kitchen and dining room may be too far apart, the bedrooms too small, or the location of the kitchen or bathroom too inconvenient. The family may need a laundry room, home office, another bathroom, an informal room for family gatherings, or an open floor plan for more light and spaciousness. An older relative may be coming to live with the family and will need a bedroom away from the rest of the family for privacy. The owner might want to combine apartments to create a bigger home.

We will first take a look at the plan arrangement of the typical historic residential Greystone, the two- and three- flat building, and the opportunities for changes in its layout. The interior of the historic Greystone is particularly amenable to change and the options for plan layouts are many. Most of these opportunities apply as well to single family and six-flat buildings, and other multi-family masonry buildings from the same historic period of the late 1800s to the 1930s.

The historic Chicago two-and three-flat Greystone is a long, narrow building, designed to fit the typical Chicago 25 foot by 125 foot lot. *(See Fig. 2)* Typically, there is one apartment on each floor, with the front entrance located on one side of the building and raised approximately one-half a floor.

From the front vestibule, there is entry to the firs[t] floor apartment and stairs to access the uppe[r] floor apartments. In each apartment, to the sid[e] of the stair in the front are the living spaces — th[e] living room and often the dining room. These ar[e] the largest rooms in the apartment and the mos[t] embellished with architectural details and cab[i]netry. The remaining rooms, smaller bedroom[s] the bathroom, and the kitchen, are arrange[d] along either side of a corridor that goes from th[e] middle to the rear of the apartment. The first floo[r] apartment may have an interior stairwell t[o] the basement; otherwise the stair is located o[n] the exterior.

Fig. 1a

Fig. 1a–1c
Examples of original
Molding Details from
a Greystone in
North Lawndale
*Photographs by
Deirdre Colgan*

Fig. 1c

## First Steps

When changing the interior plan of the historic Greystone, several existing conditions and city regulations need to be considered:

### Structural walls

In the historic Greystone, most interior walls are not structural, *i.e.*, they do not support the building and may be removed. The structural walls are usually parallel to the exterior side walls of the building and are, typically, the walls between the corridor and bedroom zone, approximately 1/3 of the way (7 to 8 feet) from one of the two sides. (See pages 64–65 for detailed drawing.) If you remove these structural walls, they need to be replaced with partial walls or columns and beams. In all cases, consulting an architect or structural engineer before removing any interior walls is highly recommended.

### Inside the walls

Some interior walls contain the plumbing stacks (hot and cold water and waste pipes) for kitchen and baths, the pipes for hot water heating, and/or heating and air-conditioning ducts. These walls need to be identified. If the renovation does not include moving these pipes and/or ducts, then these walls should not be removed. All walls are likely to have some electric, phone and perhaps cable lines. These can be readily rerouted by a professional. (See pages 78–83 for detailed drawings.)

In every older building, there may well be "surprises" in your walls that no one could foresee. In any renovation of an older building, expect the unexpected and budget accordingly. If a building has been modified over the years, it may be difficult to determine with confidence whether or not the walls contain pipes and ductwork, or to easily document the extent and type of prior repairs. When there are doubts about what exists in the property, it is helpful to consult a professional to determine what is present and to plan for the future.

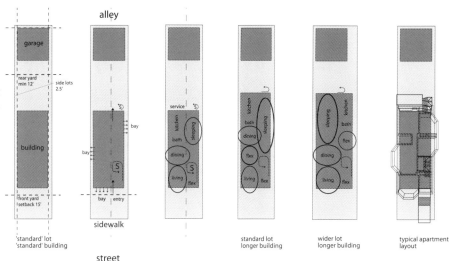

### City regulations and building codes

The City of Chicago's (or your local municipality's) regulations and building codes are key considerations when you make any alterations to your Greystone. For instance, building codes typically specify minimum room sizes; natural lighting and ventilation requirements; plumbing, heating, and HVAC systems requirements; stair design and location; minimum widths for corridors; and distance to a means of egress to the outdoors for emergencies. (See pages 90–92 for detailed information.)

### Budget

The budget for the renovation is another key factor in the decision about what types and how many changes to make. Renovation of a Greystone can be done all at once, or can be staged to accomplish the renovation over time and spread out the cost. Renovations often mean that the apartment or building may not be habitable for at least some part of the renovation project, and the cost of alternative accommodations should be considered in the budget. Even smaller projects, such as modernizing a bathroom or kitchen, may make these spaces non-functional for several weeks and require alternative arrangements.

With these issues in mind, we present alternatives to the current arrangement of a Greystone building. The following case study offers three illustrative options among many alternatives.

*Fig. 2*
Typical Layouts of Greystone Apartments
From S. Haar,
*Greystone as Type* page 96
R.M. Feldman
and J. Wheaton, (Eds)
*The Chicago Greystone in Historic North Lawndale,*
Chicago: City
Design Center, 2006

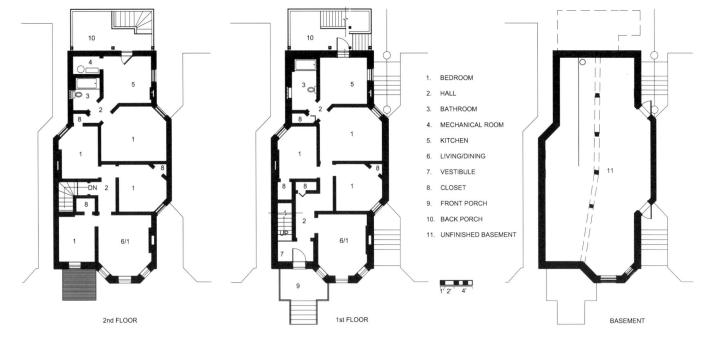

2nd FLOOR       1st FLOOR       BASEMENT

1. BEDROOM
2. HALL
3. BATHROOM
4. MECHANICAL ROOM
5. KITCHEN
6. LIVING/DINING
7. VESTIBULE
8. CLOSET
9. FRONT PORCH
10. BACK PORCH
11. UNFINISHED BASEMENT

1' 2'  4'

*Fig. 3*
Existing Layout
*Measured drawings by*
*Deirdre Colgan*
*and Adam Ariano*

## Case Study

In the Summer of 2006, Landon Bone Baker Architects (LBBA) in collaboration with the City Design Center were asked by Neighborhood Housing Services (NHS) of Chicago to design alternative renovation scenarios for a two-flat Greystone on South Spaulding Avenue in the City's North Lawndale neighborhood. Three different scenarios were developed and are described below, including the potential advantages and disadvantages of each layout. NHS of Chicago selected Scenario 2 for development as a model home for its Historic Chicago Greystone Initiative®.

## Scenario 1: Maintain or Restore Traditional Plan Layout

Scenario 1 restores each apartment as close as reasonably possible to its original layout. However, the existing plan layout of this Spaulding Avenue two-flat had been renovated previously. Had the building not been rehabbed, most of the existing walls could have been maintained or repaired if necessary. Unfortunately, in its existing condition, the apartments were maze-like and the interior was stripped of all historic details. *(See Fig. 3 )*

The renovation to restore a traditional plan layout includes relocating walls to approximate the building as originally constructed, adding closets, and modernizing the kitchen. The bath-

room is moved to its original, central location and modernized. The windows on the rear wall are restored to their original locations and size, and transom windows are restored above the interior doors for increased natural lighting and ventilation. Because the Spaulding Avenue house was shorter than a typical Greystone, there was no formal dining room in the front, rather a large eat-in kitchen in the rear. This arrangement is maintained in the renovation scheme. *(See Fig. 4 )*

*Advantages*

If in the original condition, the historic details and cabinetry could be saved and the interior preserved.
This scheme sustains the formal entertaining space in front and the private spaces in the back of each flat.
It provides privacy for individual spaces.
It is potentially the least costly option if the building is in good condition.

*Disadvantages*

The rooms in the rear of the house, especially the bedrooms are small.
Due to the close proximity of adjacent houses, natural lighting is compromised in all but the front and rear.
The emphasis on privacy decreases the experience of spaciousness.

• Unlike the case study two-flat, had this been a longer Greystone building, the dining room and kitchen would have been inconveniently separated, with the dining room in the front of the building and the kitchen in the rear.

## Scenario 2: Reorganize the Plan Layout of the Two-flat

Scenario 2 substantially reorganizes the layout of the traditional Greystone two-flat. The stair system is straightened and the hallway is repositioned to one side to allow a view straight through the entire apartment. The living spaces are moved to the rear of each apartment and organized in an open space plan with the kitchen and bathroom relocated in between the living and dining rooms. The windows in the rear walls of both apartments are increased in size for more natural lighting and views of the rear garden. The first floor apartment's space is increased by duplexing down to the basement and adding two bedrooms, a bathroom, and a flexible, multi-purpose room in the lower level.

Increased closet and storage space is added in both of the flats. In the rearrangement of the second floor flat, a modest size space is located next to the front bedroom that could be used as a study or nursery. *(See Fig. 5)*

This is only one example of options for reorganizing the plan layout of a two-flat while maintaining two distinct apartments. In a longer two-flat building, for example, one larger and one smaller apartment could be created by dividing the first floor into a small front apartment and the second floor apartment duplexed down to the rear of the first floor to add additional space. In lieu of a total gut rehab, it also is possible to maintain much of the traditional layout yet achieve a similar duplex apartment on the first and basement floors. Selectively removing bedroom walls on the first floor will provide a more open plan.

*Fig. 4*
Restore Original Layout
*Drawings by Deirdre Colgan and Adam Ariano*

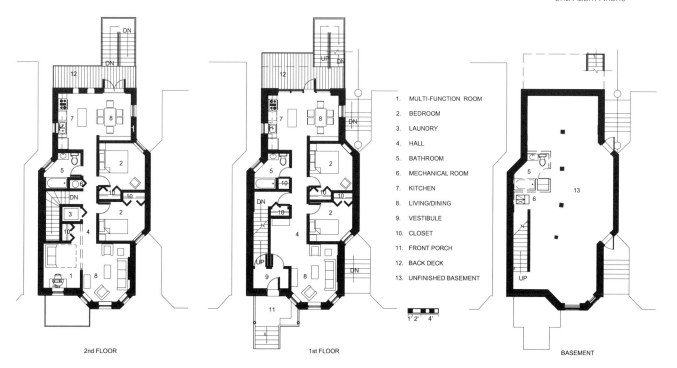

1. MULTI-FUNCTION ROOM
2. BEDROOM
3. LAUNDRY
4. HALL
5. BATHROOM
6. MECHANICAL ROOM
7. KITCHEN
8. LIVING/DINING
9. VESTIBULE
10. CLOSET
11. FRONT PORCH
12. BACK DECK
13. UNFINISHED BASEMENT

2nd FLOOR          1st FLOOR          BASEMENT

*Advantages*

- Repositioning the hallway to one side and straightening the stair allows for larger rooms.
- The open space plan gives the perception of greater spaciousness by allowing a view through the apartment and access to natural lighting.
- The kitchen is conveniently located next to dining area.
- The larger apartment's layout provides flexibility of use; *e.g.,* the spaces adjacent to the kitchen can be used interchangeably as the living room or dining room; the front room on the first floor may be used as a bedroom, home office, den or other function; and the central space on the lower level, as noted above, can be used for multiple purposes.

*Disadvantages*

- The open space plan provides less privacy, especially for sound transmission.
- While the location of the bedrooms on two floors provides for diverse household arrangements in the larger apartment, it may not be ideal for families with young children; dampness or water seepage could be a concern in the

basement rooms; and bedroom windows do not provide for as much natural lighting and view opportunities.

- In the second floor apartment, the living and dining room area occupy less space than the original layout because of the increased size of the bedrooms.
- This scheme requires a gut renovation, hence is a more costly rehab option.

## Scenario 3: Convert to a Single Family House

For people interested in a historic Greystone, but needing a larger home, the two-flat should not be overlooked. The two floors can be joined together using the existing front staircase, or by repositioning the stair to the middle of the house. Scenario 3 reorganizes the building's existing floor plan to create a large, multipurpose home. The first floor plan is dedicated to living spaces, while the upper and basement levels are designed for bedrooms and multi-purpose rooms. The first floor bath is converted to a powder room and the kitchen modernized. A second bath is added to the second floor and basement levels,

*Fig.5*
Reorganize the
2-Flat Layout
*Drawings by Deirdre Colgan
and Adam Ariano*

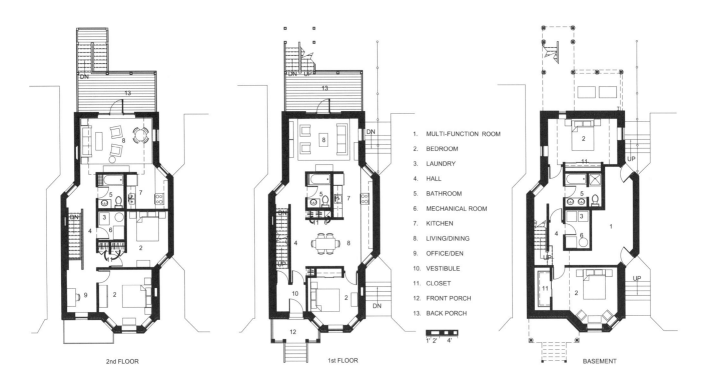

1.  MULTI-FUNCTION ROOM
2.  BEDROOM
3.  LAUNDRY
4.  HALL
5.  BATHROOM
6.  MECHANICAL ROOM
7.  KITCHEN
8.  LIVING/DINING
9.  OFFICE/DEN
10. VESTIBULE
11. CLOSET
12. FRONT PORCH
13. BACK PORCH

2nd FLOOR

1st FLOOR

BASEMENT

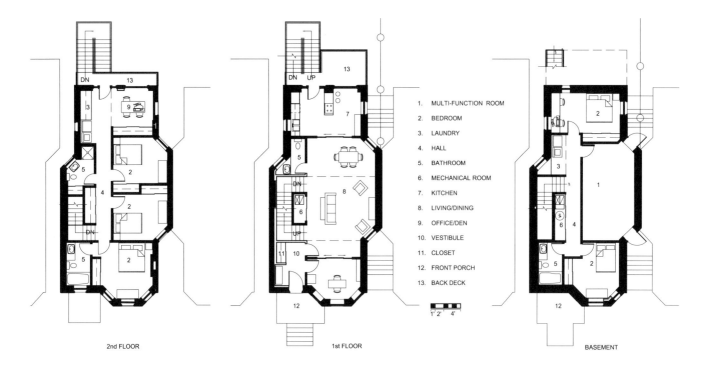

1. MULTI-FUNCTION ROOM
2. BEDROOM
3. LAUNDRY
4. HALL
5. BATHROOM
6. MECHANICAL ROOM
7. KITCHEN
8. LIVING/DINING
9. OFFICE/DEN
10. VESTIBULE
11. CLOSET
12. FRONT PORCH
13. BACK DECK

2nd FLOOR          1st FLOOR          BASEMENT

and a laundry room to the second floor. As in the second scenario, the windows in the rear walls of the first and second floors are increased in size for more natural lighting and views of the rear garden. *(See Fig. 6)*

*Advantages*
· There is a clear separation of living and sleeping spaces.
· The first floor open space plan is very spacious, allowing for large gatherings, a view from front to back, and access to natural lighting.
· The dining and kitchen spaces are conveniently located next to each other.
· The separation of the sleeping and multi-purpose rooms on two floors provides flexibility of uses. For example, the rooms on one floor may be used by the parents and young children, while the other floor by older children. As in Scenario 2, the bedrooms could also be used for home office, den, or other functions; and the central space on the lower level, as a workshop, exercise room or other purposes.

*Disadvantages*
· As in any open space plan, there is less privacy, especially for sound transmission.
· As in any scheme that duplexes down to the basement, dampness or water seepage could be a concern and the windows in the basement rooms do not provide for as much natural lighting and views out.
· This scenario, as the second scenario, requires a gut renovation. This is a particularly costly rehab because there is no rental income from a separate first or second floor apartment to assist in defraying housing costs.
· Deconverting to a single family home may also have an impact on the appraised value of the building.

There are many other possible arrangements to reorganize a two-flat into a single family home. In the third scenario above, the basement need not be renovated and would still provide a large, three or four bedroom house. An even more modest renovation is possible if the building is in good condition. The stair system can be kept in its original position and the doors to the two apartments eliminated to connect the first and second floors. Selective removal of the bedroom walls on the first floor will open the plan to a generous living space. On the second floor, the appliances and cabinets in the rear second floor kitchen could be removed and a closet and door installed to provide a third bedroom. The front open space also can be converted to a bedroom by adding a wall, door and closet, or left as is for multiple purposes such as a study or family room.

*Fig. 6*
Convert 2-Flat to Single Family House
*Drawings by Deirdre Colgan and Adam Ariano*

### Details

In addition to the many more possible layouts illustrated above, there are design details that can add to the livability of the space. For instance, you might consider:

· Removing and re-using historical details, trim, cabinets and fixtures in new locations that better fit your needs

· A flexible alternative to a full wall would be no wall at all between spaces, or pocket doors to create more alternatives to open or close the floor plan

· Partial-height walls (with and without glass above) for capturing borrowed natural light from other spaces

· Double-height spaces that can be introduced by removing the floor between two spaces

· Skylights or Sola-Tubes® installed in the roof to add natural lighting to this double-story space or to an upper floor space

### The Value of a Greystone

A sensitive renovation of an historic building like a Chicago Greystone can result in a practical update for contemporary living, but it takes work and planning. Affordability is one consideration that makes it worth the effort. Rehabilitation is a cost-effective strategy — the cost of repairing an older home is significantly less expensive than new construction, especially when considering the quality of the building. Rehabilitation can also reduce operating costs of the building through the use of energy-efficient appliances, green technologies and other energy-saving improvements. Preservation of multi-family residential buildings adds to their affordability, by providing owners with rental income to defray housing costs and renters with quality apartments. The spirit of historic preservation is found in the committed individuals who see the value of the beauty of these architectural treasures and their role in the continuity of community heritage and sense of place.

# Preserving the Stone

The gray limestone façade gives the Chicago Greystone a grand and noble appearance and is the defining feature of this building type. It is worthwhile for Greystone owners to do what is necessary to restore, clean, and maintain the integrity and beauty of this historic limestone masonry. In this chapter we will discuss the history and distinctive quality of the limestone as a building material, the types of soiling or damage that commonly affect historic exterior limestone masonry, and the variety of options for cleaning, repair, and maintenance.

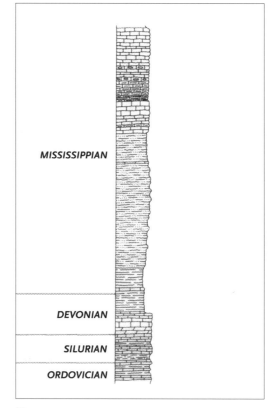

Fig. 2

*Fig. 1*
*Sedimentary deposits in Illinois. The letters indicate the ages of the rocks: Pre-C= Precambrian, C=Cambrian, O=Ordovician, S=Silurian, D=Devonian, M=Mississippian, P=Pennsylvanian, K=Cretaceous, and T=Tertiary. The Joliet-Lemont limestone quarries are located where the Silurian deposits are found near the surface. Courtesy of Illinois State Geological Survey.*

*Fig. 2*
*Indiana limestone was formed in the Mississippian epoch. Courtesy Indiana Geological Survey.*

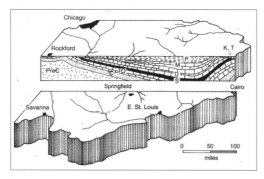

Fig. 1

## About the Limestone

Limestone is primarily composed of materials that came from the sea — grains of calcite (calcium carbonate) from shell fragments and skeletal parts of organisms. Limestone in the bedrock of Illinois was formed 400 million years ago, during the Silurian geological epoch, when this land mass was located south of the equator and covered by a shallow tropical sea. In southern Indiana there are large deposits of limestone found near the Earth's surface that were formed during the Mississippian epoch, about 300 million years ago. The Indiana limestone is true limestone, consisting of almost one hundred percent calcite; the majority of the calcium in the Silurian deposits found in Illinois was replaced throughout time with magnesium, transforming the stone into what is technically dolomite, though this stone is still often called limestone. *(See Fig. 1 and 2)*

Taking advantage of the rich mineral resources found in the surrounding areas, the stone industry in Chicago was strong throughout the nineteenth and much of the twentieth century. Demand for stone building materials in Chicago grew particularly high after the Chicago Fire of 1871. Originally, the majority of cut limestone used by Chicago builders came from quarries in Illinois — particularly from the Joliet-Lemont area. When it was discovered that limestone quarried in the Bedford area of Indiana was more durable and of a higher quality, Indiana limestone became favored as a building material. Illinois quarries shifted to producing crushed limestone aggregate. By the end of the nineteenth century most of Chicago's supply of cut limestone for buildings came from the Bedford area of Indiana. *(See Fig. 3)*

It is easy to tell the difference between Joliet limestone and Indiana limestone, because the two types of limestone weather differently. After years of exposure to the elements Joliet-Lemont limestone tends to weather a yellow/tan color due to high iron content. The Water Tower, one of the few buildings to have survived the Chicago Fire is

*Fig. 3*

a highly visible example of a building clad in Joliet limestone. Indiana Limestone maintains a gray hue and also tends not to peel as much as Joliet-Lemont limestone does. The Chicago Tribune Tower was built with Indiana Limestone. It is possible that the limestone façades on some of the Chicago Greystones were built with Joliet-Lemont limestone, though Indiana limestone is probably the material that was used for most Greystones. *(See Fig. 4 and 5)*

*Fig. 4*          *Fig. 5*

The nature of limestone allows for cutting and finishing in many different styles. The surface can be left rough. Machines, such as saws, grinders, or planers can be used to give cut stone a smooth finish; or machines can also be used to cut uniform grooves in the surface of the stone, giving it a machine-tooled finish. High quality limestone can also be carved into intricate, ornate shapes. A variety of styles of limestone finishing can be found on Chicago Greystones, and often multiple styles are juxtaposed on the same building.

## Soiling and Deterioration of Greystone Façades

In order to determine what types of information and resources would be most useful to Greystone owners, the City Design Center conducted an analysis of Greystone rehabilitation projects in which Neighborhood Housing Services of Chicago (NHS) staff had assisted. Researchers looked at reports of 75 Lawndale Greystone rehabilitation projects completed by NHS over the past ten years and found that 70% of the buildings required repairs to the limestone masonry. Indiana limestone in particular has a reputation for durability, but after a century of exposure to weather and pollution the façade of your Greystone is likely showing signs of wear.

This section of the guide is intended to provide you with information that will help you assess what types of dirt or damage you might find on the exterior masonry of your Greystone and decide among the options for cleaning or repair. Bear in mind that the use of inappropriate cleaning or repair methods can actually do more harm than good, so the risks and likely benefits of any such project must be carefully weighed, and in most cases it is best to seek the services of professionals experienced in working with historic masonry.

## Cleaning Projects

*Types of Soiling*

The first step in preparing for a cleaning project is to determine what type of dirt or soiling has accumulated on your Greystone.

· Biological Growth

This can include mold and mildew and also vines or the pieces of plant matter that are left stuck to the wall when vines have been removed. Often biological growth is soft and green and relatively easy to clean off, though once the biological material has been removed a "shadow" or stain can remain on the surface of the stone.

Atmospheric Pollution
· Pollutants in the air can leave deposits on exterior masonry that accumulate over time. Dirt or soot from pollution is often hardened and black or dark grey in color. *(See Fig. 6)*

· Staining
As mentioned above, stains can include grey shadows left behind when biological growth is removed. Stains can also be caused by the weathering of metal anchors on the stone or metal decorative elements on the façade; you might find rust stains from iron or green stains from the weathering of copper. Previous attempts at cleaning the stone using improper methods may have also left the stains, some of which may be impossible to remove.

· Paint
Some Greystones may have been painted, and due to the porous nature of the stone may require a new coat every three to four years. Any paint used on limestone needs to be vapor permeable, so that the stone can "breathe." Otherwise, water can get trapped beneath the paint and cause the stone to deteriorate. You may need to remove paint that is not vapor permeable.

*Cleaning Methods*
Your purpose for cleaning and goal for cleanliness should be determined before undertaking a cleaning project. It may not be necessary or feasible to get the building to look brand new; you may just need to clean to a level where the soiling is not damaging the building.

It is important to identify the nature of the material to be removed, because you will want to clean the masonry by the most appropriate method. The best method of cleaning will be the gentlest method that will make the surface cleaner without damaging the stone, harming the environment or putting anyone's health at risk.

Methods for cleaning historic masonry generally fall into three categories: water, chemical, and abrasive cleaning methods. Other methods, such as laser cleaning are being studied, but are not yet practical options for most residential projects. Any cleaning method should be tested in an inconspicuous area in order to determine its effectiveness and ensure that it will not further damage the masonry.

· Water Cleaning Methods
Water cleaning methods are the gentlest means of cleaning historic limestone and likely also the most economical and practical. There are three types of water cleaning methods: soaking, pressure washing, and steam.

Soaking involves spraying or misting the stone with water over a period of time (several days to a week) using an apparatus such as a punctured hose or pipe set on a scaffold. This type of cleaning is most effective in removing heavy deposits of soot.

Pressure washing can be very damaging to the masonry if not done carefully and without taking into consideration the extent of deterioration before cleaning. When pressure washing, start with a very low pressure and increase pressure incrementally if necessary. (Do not exceed 400 P.S.I.)

Steam cleaning is a particularly effective way of gently cleaning acid sensitive stone such as limestone and is a good alternative to chemical cleaning. The steam is applied to the masonry at an extremely low pressure, using much less water than conventional pressure washing. The heat and moisture combine to loosen built-up dirt and can also be effective in the removal of dried-up plant materials affixed to the masonry. This method is especially useful for removing dirt deposits from ornately carved stone.

All water-cleaning methods are usually combined with gentle hand scrubbing using a natural or synthetic bristle brush and a final water rinse. Before undertaking any water cleaning method, a full inspection of the soundness of all mortar-joints should be performed, and the overall water tightness of your structure including window and door openings should be checked. Furthermore, all water cleaning projects must be avoided during times when frost or freezing is expected.

· Chemical Cleaning Methods
Chemical cleaning is harsher then water methods, but may be necessary to remove extensive soiling from soot, paint, stains, caulking compounds, oils, and any other non-water soluble material. Chemical cleaners are acidic, alkaline, or organic compounds that react with the dirt or the stone itself.

Acid cleaners should generally be avoided in cleaning limestone because acid will react with the calcite in the stone, and will likely lead to more damage.

Alkaline cleaners are a better choice for limestone cleaning projects. The process of cleaning masonry using alkaline cleaners involves pre-wetting the stone with water, applying the chemical and allowing it to set for a period of time, and then rinsing with water. It may be necessary to follow this initial rinse with a slightly acidic wash to neutralize the stone's surface, and then rinse again with water.

Organic compounds include aromatic hydrocarbons and chlorinated hydrocarbons. These solvents are often used for paint removal.

Chemical cleaning requires careful consideration, not only of the damage it may cause to the limestone, but also of potential environmental and health hazards. A professional should be consulted before undertaking any chemical cleaning project.

· Mechanical and Abrasive Cleaning Methods
It is not recommended that mechanical or abrasive cleaning methods be used on historic limestone masonry. These methods include high-pressure water blasting, sand blasting, and the use of grit blasters, grinders and sanding discs. These methods remove the outer surface of the masonry and can also damage the mortar.

**Repair Projects**
The limestone façades of Chicago's historic Greystones have been exposed to a number of threats over the decades. A very common cause of cracks and spalling (peeling of the surface) is water penetration followed by cyclic freezing of water near the surface during cold weather. Expansion of the water as it freezes splits the stone. Buildup of environmental pollutants can also cause the stone to deteriorate. A chemical reaction takes place between the calcite in the stone, water, and sulfuric acid (in acid rain) or sulfur dioxide gas (in polluted air), and the mineral gypsum is formed. The gypsum crust eventually blisters and peels off, and the stone surface crumbles *(See Fig. 7)*. Other causes of cracking or deterioration of historic limestone façades include, wind erosion, thermal expansion and contraction, and previous attempts at cleaning or repair of the limestone using improper methods.

*Fig. 6*
Patterns of staining on this masonry are caused by the patterns of rain water washing over the rusticated cut limestone. Areas that are most exposed to rainwater appear cleanest because the rain washes away dirt and soot along with small layers of the limestone itself. Staining appears more prominently in areas that are somewhat protected from the rain.

Fig. 7
Formation of gypsum crust has caused spalling and deterioration of the stone.

Fig. 8
Water penetration followed by freeze/ thaw cycling has caused the mortar joints to split, which has then led to cracking through the stone.

Fig. 7

*Methods of Repair*

This section is intended to give you an overview of the options available for repair of damage to the façade of your Greystone. The consultation and services of specialists is required to properly assess the causes and appropriate methods for repair of historic masonry.

· Patching Cracks
  Minute cracks in limestone can be repaired by using a router to grind the opening to one-half inch and filling with a polymer-modified mortar. Pressure-injection of epoxy can sometimes be used to fill larger cracks.

· Mortar Repair
  Sound mortar joints play an important role in keeping the structure water-tight and preventing deterioration of the limestone. Damaged mortar needs to be removed (to a depth of three-quarters to one inch), preferably using hand tools to prevent damage to the surrounding stones. The joint can then be re-pointed with a high calcium lime mortar. *(See Fig. 8)*

· Replacement
  Stone that has been severely damaged and cannot be repaired or patched may require replacement. This is certainly not a do-it-yourself project; you will need to hire a skilled mason to perform the removal and replacement of the

stone. It is important that you find a replacement stone that is as similar as possible to the adjacent stones in appearance and character. If your Greystone was built using Indiana limestone you will have an easier time finding a suitable replacement stone than if it was built using Joliet-Lemont limestone. The Indiana limestone quarries are still actively producing cut limestone. Minnesota limestone and Silverdale limestone from Kansas are somewhat similar in character to Joliet limestone and may be a suitable substitute. Salvaged limestone from demolished buildings may also be a source for replacement stone. It is not recommended that Greystone owners replace blocks of limestone with stone substitutes or any material other than limestone.

**Maintenance**

Along with cleaning and repairing the façade of your Greystone it is important to do what you can to prevent further damage.

Water penetration is a key cause of damage to exterior limestone, and so it is imperative that Greystone owners ensure the water-tightness of the structure. You can keep water out by ensuring the soundness of mortar joints, windows, and doors and installing gutter and flashing systems, making sure that all water from downspouts is diverted away from the surface of the stone. Weep holes in the stone veneer itself can also help to allow water that has entered the wall to escape. *(See Fig. 9)*

Fig. 8

Moisture can also seep in from the soil below the wall. This is called "rising damp." Grading the soil to cause water to flow away from the building can prevent "rising damp."

Additionally, you can prevent some of the damage that might be caused by cyclic freezing and thawing of moisture in the stone by maintaining a steady warm temperature on the interior of your Greystone during the winter months.

*Fig. 9*

*Fig. 9*
Replacement stones in this wall have been fitted with weep holes that allow water that seeps into the wall to escape.

## For More Information

In this chapter we have provided a brief overview of the types of damage that may affect the façade of your Greystone and some options for cleaning and repair. As you prepare to undertake such projects, however, you will likely want to seek more detailed information.

The U.S. National Park Service's Technical Preservation Services provides excellent resources for individuals involved in preservation and restoration of historic buildings through a series of pamphlets called Preservation Briefs. The Preservation Briefs most relevant to Greystone façade cleaning and repair projects include: Preservation Brief 01: "Assessing Cleaning and Water-Repellent Treatments," Preservation Brief 02: "Repointing Mortar Joints in Historic Masonry Buildings," Preservation Brief 06: "Dangers of Abrasive Cleaning to Historic Buildings," Preservation Brief 16: "The Use of Substitute Materials on Historic Building Exteriors," Preservation Brief 38: "Removing Graffiti from Historic Masonry," and Preservation Brief 39: "Holding the Line: Controlling Unwanted Moisture in Historic Buildings." The entire series of Preservation Briefs is available for free online at http://www.nps.gov/hps/tps/briefs/presbhom. htm.

The Landmarks Preservation Council of Illinois (http://www.landmarks.org) provides resources for owners and supporters of historic buildings in Illinois. Among the publications available for order from their website is a text about the history and preservation of Joliet-Lemont limestone masonry: *Preservation of an Historic Building Material: Joliet-Lemont Limestone* by James C. Bradbury. This booklet includes detailed recommendations for cleaning and repair projects.

The Indiana Limestone Institute of America, Inc. (ILIA) (http://www.iliai.com) is a trade association of Indiana Limestone quarriers and fabricators. ILIA is a great resource for more information about the Indiana Limestone industry, the characteristics of the stone itself and how to care for it. They offer a number of free publications that Greystone owners may find useful, such as *How to Avoid Small Area Stains and Blemishes, Repair Booklet,* and the *Indiana Limestone Handbook.* ILIA also provides information and referral services and welcomes questions from the public by phone (812.275.4426) or by contacting their website at iliai.com.

Some of the best sources of information to help you make decisions about restoration of your limestone masonry may be other Greystone owners in your neighborhood who have undertaken similar projects and, of course, professionals experienced in the cleaning and repair of historic masonry. Neighborhood Housing Services of Chicago can help you to locate such individuals.

Limestone restoration requires careful consideration and well-informed decision-making, so you will likely want to consult a variety of information resources before undertaking any project. The limestone façade is what makes your Chicago Greystone special, and it is important that this masonry be cleaned, repaired, and maintained by the best means possible.

# The Façade, Improved

Center bay often fixed with transom window above

Typical double (or single) hung thermopane windows

Cleaned, restored Greystone façade

Parkway tree

Ornamental tree

Flashing

Beadboard ceiling

Exterior lighting

Full or ¾ lite vision door with transom above, typically with house number

Wood columns and canopy, with decorative steel railings, painted

Painted wood risers and treads

Infill lattice panels

Decorative railings

Concrete starter step

Permeable pavers

Restored or new concrete sidewalk

# The Porch

Sheet metal flashing into
masonry joint, soft seal

Roofing shingles: 3:12 slope minimum
for shingles without membrane below
or metal standing seam

Cedar beadboard, painted or sealed

6 inch x 6 inch wood post (cedar); add detail
with chamfers, trim, painted

Decorative steel newel post, infill
replicate "spirit" of existing railings
found in neighborhood, painted

Painted wood steps and risers; (add fine
sand to paint to add slip resistance to treads)

Reinforced concrete starter step,
slope to drain

Permeable paving (or concrete)

Pier foundation for heavier loads,
set to below frost line

Post hole footing set to below frost line

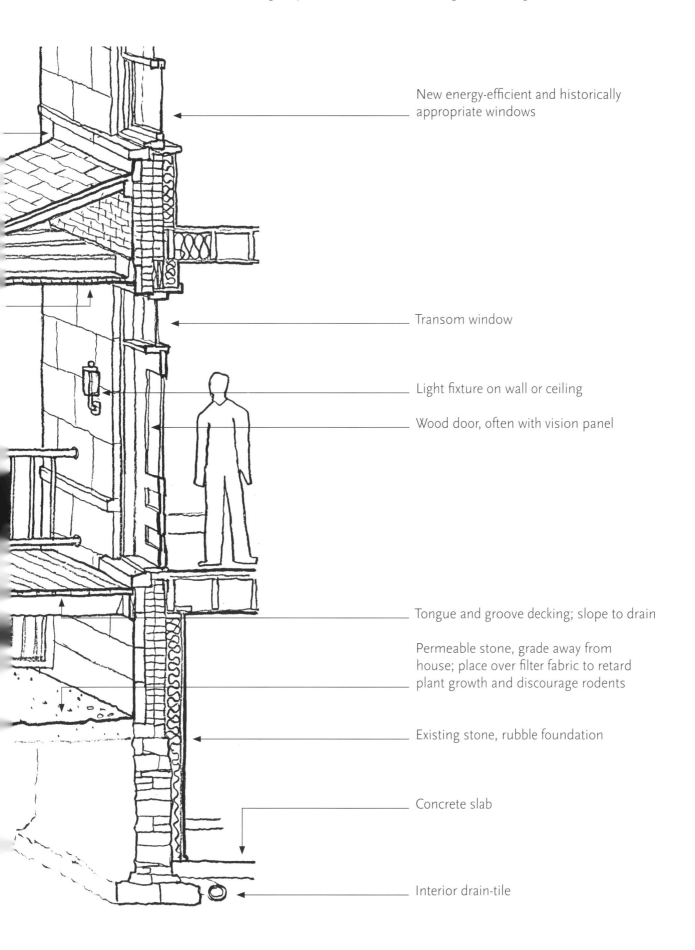

New energy-efficient and historically appropriate windows

Transom window

Light fixture on wall or ceiling

Wood door, often with vision panel

Tongue and groove decking; slope to drain

Permeable stone, grade away from house; place over filter fabric to retard plant growth and discourage rodents

Existing stone, rubble foundation

Concrete slab

Interior drain-tile

# Focus Front Façade:

Upgrades and Improvements

*Photographs by*
*Deirdre Colgan*

Wood awning structure

Wood ballustrades are susceptible
to rot, not sturdy, and are inelegant
if sized to meet codes

Full lite door with transom

Decorative steel fence

Center picture window with transom

Beadboard ceiling

Typical double-hung window

Flashing

Do not use steel columns

Wood columns

Do use decorative steel guardrails

# Focus Front Façade:

Upgrades and Improvements *continued*

**Front Door Options**

Options depend upon the size of the
door opening

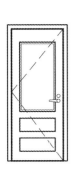

3/4 Lite

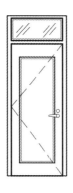

Full Lite

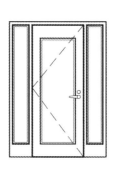

Full Lite
with Transom

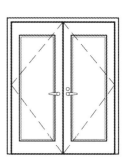

Full Lite with Lites

Full Lite Double Door

**Window Options**

Bay Windows

Upper Story Windows

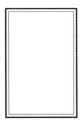

Fixed

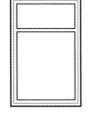

Fixed with
Transom

Single-hung

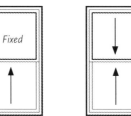

Double-hung

Basement Windows

Awning

Hopper

Pivoting

Sliding

*Note:* It should be noted that care should be taken in the selection of window and door profiles to be compatible with the building's design and proportions. On the whole, primary concern should be taken to restore or replace openings in façades facing the public way/ street with profiles that would have matched the original. This would include use of double-hung windows, fixed units with transoms at center bays, and entry doors with half or three quarter glazed units.

Original windows were single pane glass in wood sash, typically painted on the exterior, with exterior attached screens/storm windows. Replacement windows are now available with insulating glass. These can now be provided as natural or shop painted wood, prefinished aluminum or integrally colored vinyl clad wood, or all aluminum or vinyl. Each have their "pros" and "cons," with the latter options being the least appropriate to a primary façade, as well as from a sustainability viewpoint.

If in doubt regarding the above, we recommend touring the adjacent neighbourhood to look at profiles, materials and colors that seem most complementary to similar buildings.

# Focus Rear Façade:

Commonly Overlooked Code Violations

Any notching in column is prohibited

Check that stair is at least 3 feet wide

Column spacing exceeds 5 feet max

Check that guardrail is at least 3 feet 6 inches above finish floor

Ballustrade spacing exceeds the 4 inch max

Column improperly affixed to concrete footing

*Photograph by
Deirdre Colgan*

## Code Violation Photos

*From left to right* (1) Columns are required to be seated and affixed to a metal connector base. (2) Improper through-bolting of column splicing. (3) Beam improperly framing into column. Column notching prohibited.
*Courtesy of Landon Bone Baker Architects*

*From left to right* (1) Column is weakened through shrinkage cracks and splitting. (2) Improper stair winders.
*Courtesy of Landon Bone Baker Architects*

## Code Compliant Photos

*From left to right* (1) Columns are seated and affixed to a metal connector base and are resting on a solid retaining wall. (2) Metal brackets affixed to the columns support the floor load. *Courtesy of Landon Bone Baker Architects*

# Focus Rear Façade:

Commonly Overlooked Code Violations *continued*

## Code Compliant Details

The following drawings are taken from the City of Chicago's *Guide to Porch and Deck Design and Construction*. The selected drawings highlight some commonly overlooked details which are key to porch code compliance. For a complete list of drawings necessary for code compliance, please refer to the City of Chicago's *Guide to Porch and Deck Design and Construction* at www.cityofchicago.org/buildings.

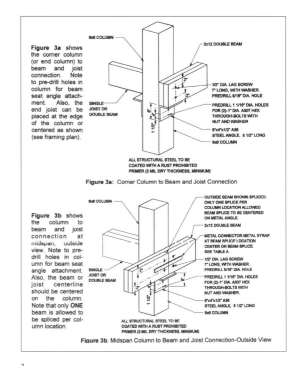

1

*From left to right* (1) Joint, Column, Beam Connection (2) Joint, Column, Beam Connection (3) Standard Footing Detail (4) Column Splice Detail (5) Railing Detail

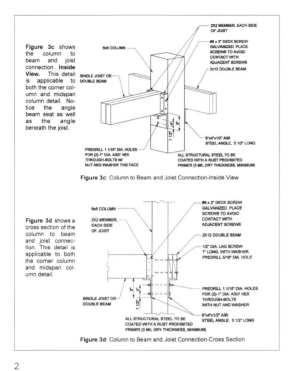

Figure 3c shows the column to beam and joist connection Inside View. This detail is applicable to both the corner column and midspan column detail. Notice the angle beam seat as well as the angle beneath the joist.

Figure 3c: Column to Beam and Joist Connection-Inside View

Figure 3d shows a cross section of the column to beam and joist connection. This detail is applicable to both the corner column and midspan column detail.

Figure 3d: Column to Beam and Joist Connection-Cross Section

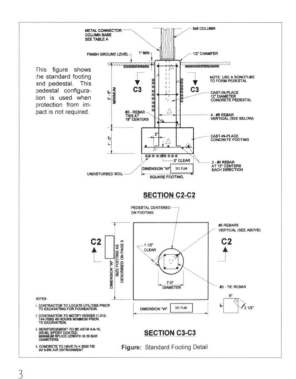

This figure shows the standard footing and pedestal. This pedestal configuration is used when protection from impact is not required.

SECTION C2-C2

SECTION C3-C3

Figure: Standard Footing Detail

2

3

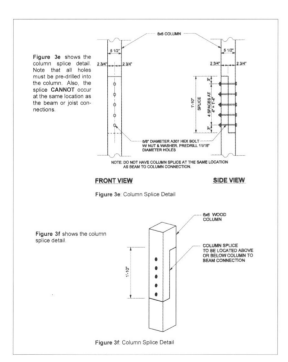

Figure 3e shows the column splice detail. Note that all holes must be pre-drilled into the column. Also, the splice CANNOT occur at the same location as the beam or joist connections.

FRONT VIEW          SIDE VIEW

Figure 3e: Column Splice Detail

Figure 3f shows the column splice detail.

Figure 3f: Column Splice Detail

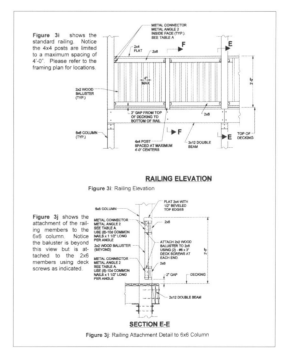

Figure 3i shows the standard railing. Notice the 4x4 posts are limited to a maximum spacing of 4'-0". Please refer to the framing plan for locations.

RAILING ELEVATION

Figure 3i: Railing Elevation

Figure 3j shows the attachment of the railing members to the 6x6 column. Notice the baluster is beyond this view but is attached to the 2x6 members using deck screws as indicated.

SECTION E-E

Figure 3j: Railing Attachment Detail to 6x6 Column

4

5

# "Opening Up"

What to remove to open up the
interior, and how to do it.

The interior structure of a typical Greystone is
fairly receptive to change; interior walls running
perpendicular to the bearing walls are generally
non-bearing, and the interior bearing wall can be
opened up by use of beams as illustrated herein.

**Header below the floor framing**

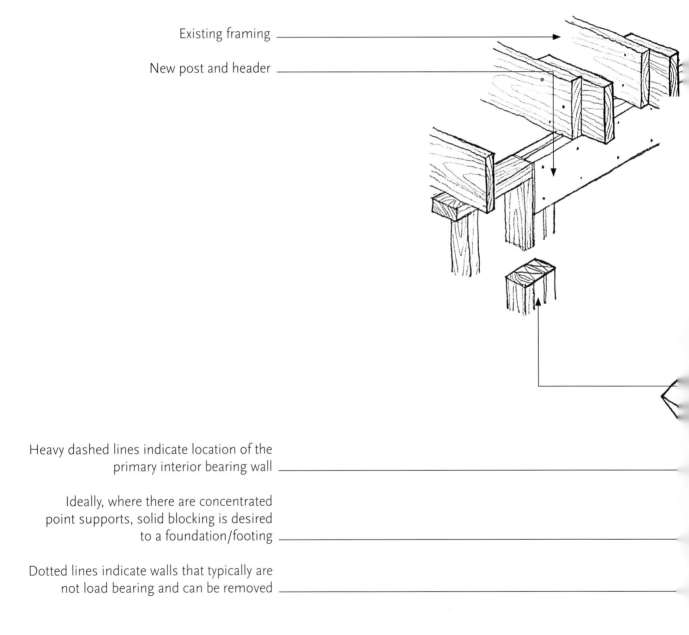

Existing framing

New post and header

Heavy dashed lines indicate location of the
primary interior bearing wall

Ideally, where there are concentrated
point supports, solid blocking is desired
to a foundation/footing

Dotted lines indicate walls that typically are
not load bearing and can be removed

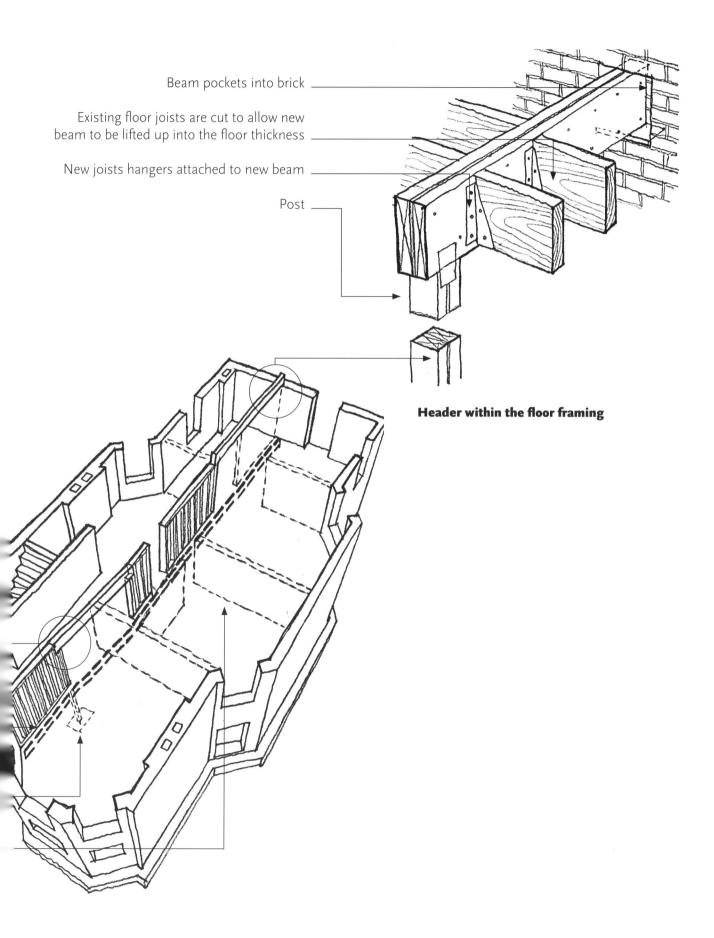

Beam pockets into brick

Existing floor joists are cut to allow new beam to be lifted up into the floor thickness

New joists hangers attached to new beam

Post

**Header within the floor framing**

# Various Masonry Openings

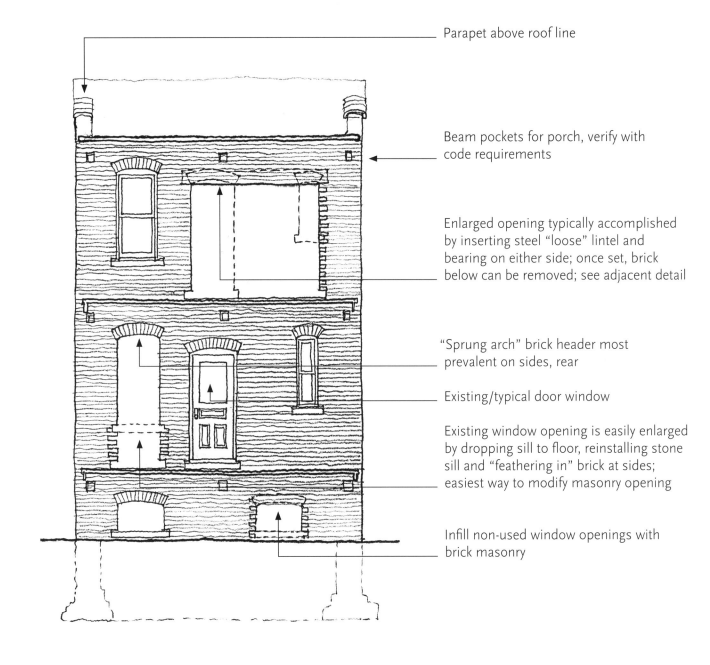

Parapet above roof line

Beam pockets for porch, verify with code requirements

Enlarged opening typically accomplished by inserting steel "loose" lintel and bearing on either side; once set, brick below can be removed; see adjacent detail

"Sprung arch" brick header most prevalent on sides, rear

Existing/typical door window

Existing window opening is easily enlarged by dropping sill to floor, reinstalling stone sill and "feathering in" brick at sides; easiest way to modify masonry opening

Infill non-used window openings with brick masonry

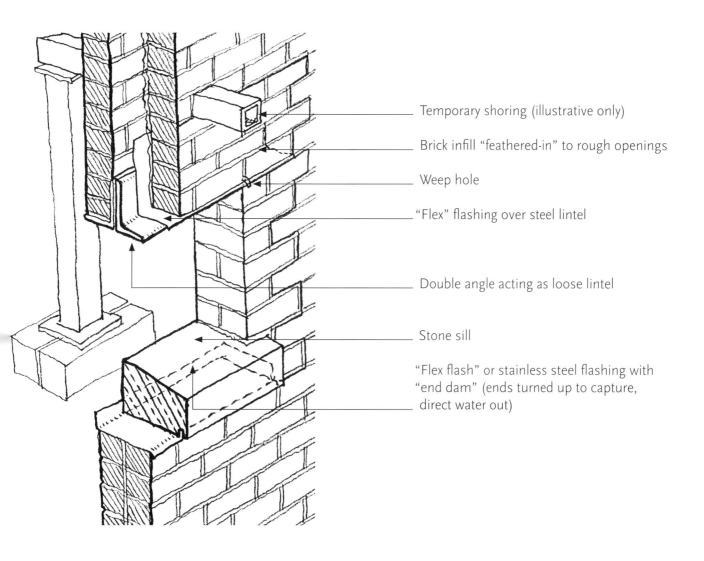

Temporary shoring (illustrative only)

Brick infill "feathered-in" to rough openings

Weep hole

"Flex" flashing over steel lintel

Double angle acting as loose lintel

Stone sill

"Flex flash" or stainless steel flashing with "end dam" (ends turned up to capture, direct water out)

# A Greystone Reborn

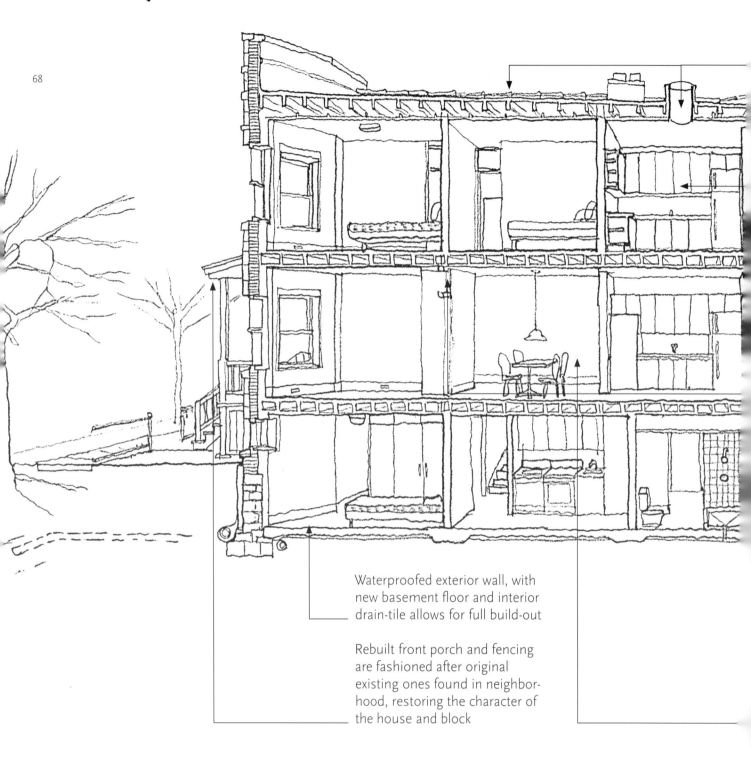

Waterproofed exterior wall, with
new basement floor and interior
drain-tile allows for full build-out

Rebuilt front porch and fencing
are fashioned after original
existing ones found in neighborhood, restoring the character of
the house and block

New reflective roof cools building while light tubes bring light into the building's interior

New kitchen/bath cores moved to interior, allowing full width access of primary living space to rear of house, with broad view to backyard

New back porch/stair configuration provides light and usable deck area for each unit; use of metal mesh within railings provides the code required safety infill and a structure to support climbing vegetation

Use of transom windows above standard doors maximizes sense of height and vision through house; can be used to enhance cross-ventilation

Condensing unit tucked out of view

Catch basin either maintained or removed

Located at the interior of each unit, dining space acknowledges use in evenings, freeing perimeter for light filled study and living spaces

# Greystone "Outback" Revisited

Parapets rebuilt, ivy removed, house tuck-pointed

New masonry opening brings daylight to units; infill of glass, doors, spandrel panels, lighting, and gutter is coordinated

The porch roof is eliminated at the top level, increasing daylight to the second floor unit and further defining the character of multiple units; (top unit is close to the sky, the lower unit is strongly connected to the ground/garden)

Columnar trees help screen inexpensive/ uncoordinated fencing, provide privacy

Stairway is pulled out into rear yard, affording a usable space on each level for sitting, cooking, dining al fresco

Air conditioning condensing unit placed under open deck, screened from view by screening used as railing infill, providing a grid work for climbing vines

Permeable walks

Railings rebuilt and compliant with historical precedents

Vegetable garden

# Interior Detailing
Contemporary Practices

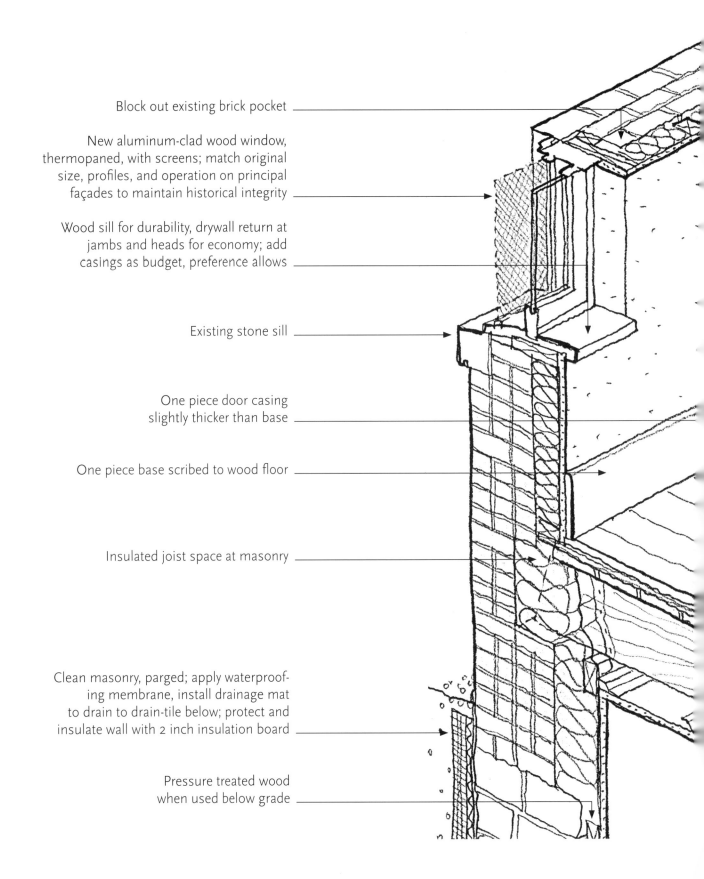

Block out existing brick pocket

New aluminum-clad wood window, thermopaned, with screens; match original size, profiles, and operation on principal façades to maintain historical integrity

Wood sill for durability, drywall return at jambs and heads for economy; add casings as budget, preference allows

Existing stone sill

One piece door casing slightly thicker than base

One piece base scribed to wood floor

Insulated joist space at masonry

Clean masonry, parged; apply waterproofing membrane, install drainage mat to drain to drain-tile below; protect and insulate wall with 2 inch insulation board

Pressure treated wood when used below grade

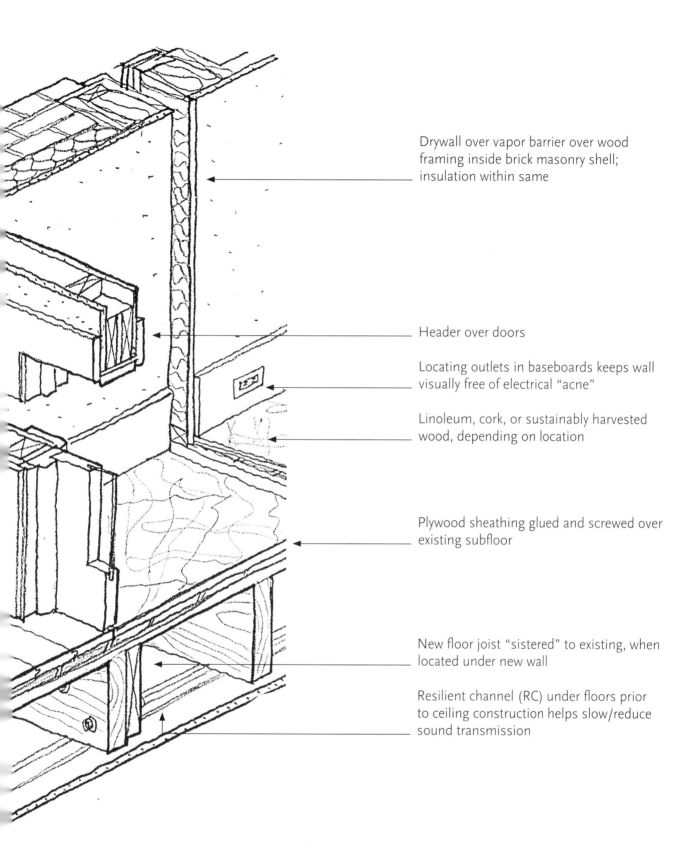

Drywall over vapor barrier over wood framing inside brick masonry shell; insulation within same

Header over doors

Locating outlets in baseboards keeps wall visually free of electrical "acne"

Linoleum, cork, or sustainably harvested wood, depending on location

Plywood sheathing glued and screwed over existing subfloor

New floor joist "sistered" to existing, when located under new wall

Resilient channel (RC) under floors prior to ceiling construction helps slow/reduce sound transmission

# Staying Dry:

Roof

Limestone coping

Soft sealant (typical at skyward exposed joints)

Through flashing

Sealant

Termination bar

Flashing (single ply membrane)

Parapet flashing (single ply membrane)

Structural wood deck

Rigid insulation board

Vapor barrier

Gypsum board

Base sheet

Batt insulation

Roof vents (through wall or through roof) to vent void space below

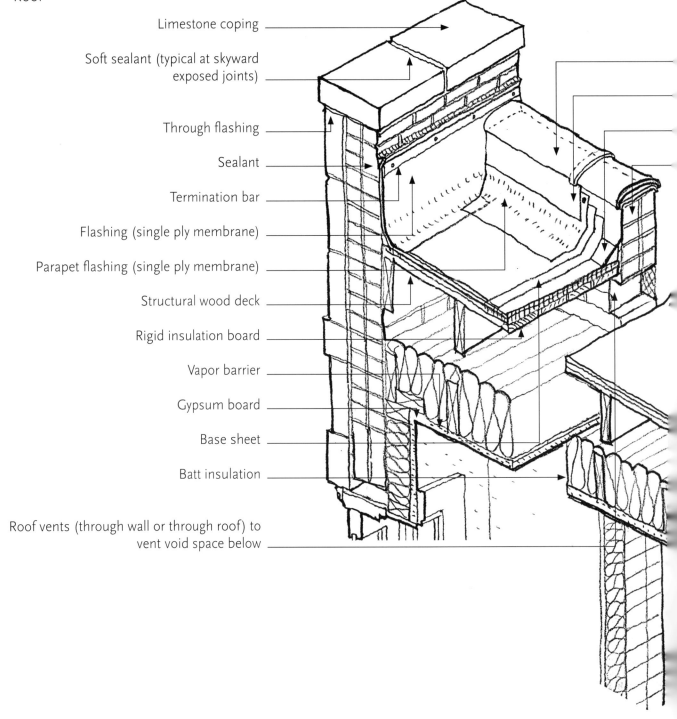

Ceramic/clay coping

Single-ply counter flashing

Cant strip

Masonry parapet wall

Slope minimum 1/4 inch per foot

1. *Roof Removal and Replacement* is the installation of a new membrane system after complete removal of all roof components above the structural deck. This generally is considered the safest and surest method to guarantee long term performance.

2. *Reroof or Recover,* is refitting the existing roof system with a new membrane cover and all related flashing, over the top of the existing roof membrane. New insulation is generally used to separate the new membrane from the existing membrane.

In general, reroofing may be successfully completed if the original roofing system is securely attached to the deck, is not significantly deteriorated, if the structural deck and insulation are in satisfactory condition, and the system does not contain excessive amounts of moisture.

3. *Roof Repair* is repair work of actual leaks and obvious deteriorated areas on an identified localized basis. Good repair work generally requires highly skilled roofing experience in defects identification and proper roofing practices.

Downspout

Gutter guard/screen

Aluminum or galvanized gutter

Gutterstrap

# Staying Dry:

Foundation

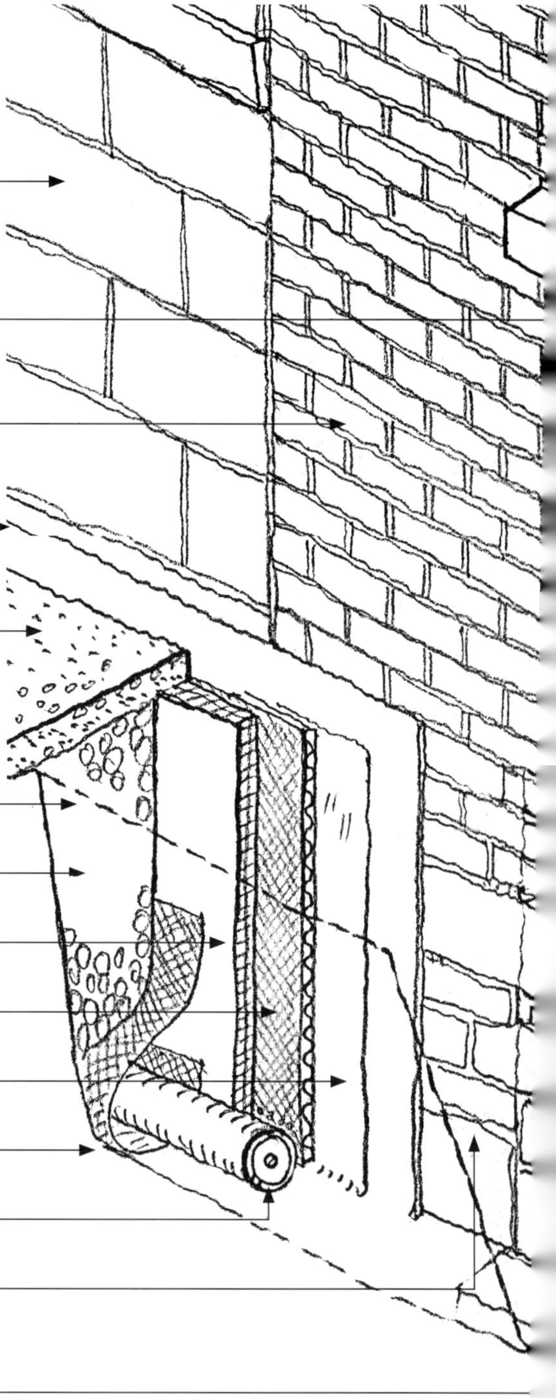

Greystone veneer

Lug sill (stone sill has extended "ears" that are locked into the masonry on either side, assisting with keeping the wall watertight)

Typically porous "Chicago common" brick masonry, tuck-pointed

Cementitious parging

6 inch stone, soil or paving, slope away from house

Dashed line indicates excavation

Crushed stone backfill, compacted

Rigid insulation

Drainage mat

Waterproofing membrane

Filter fabric

Drain-tile, place holes down

Mortar joints

Clean and dry out masonry, rake out soft joints

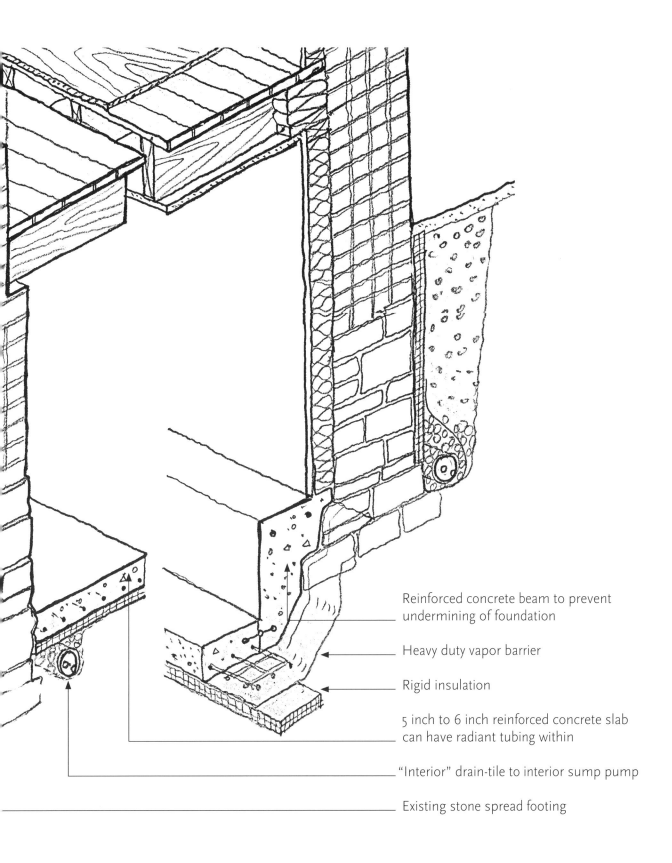

Reinforced concrete beam to prevent undermining of foundation

Heavy duty vapor barrier

Rigid insulation

5 inch to 6 inch reinforced concrete slab can have radiant tubing within

"Interior" drain-tile to interior sump pump

Existing stone spread footing

# Basics of
# Mechanical Systems

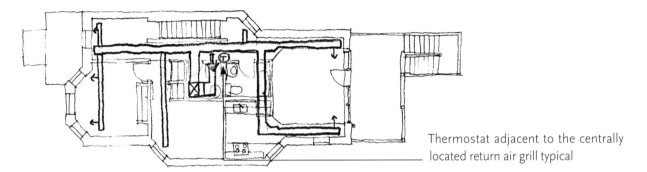

Thermostat adjacent to the centrally located return air grill typical

**Second Floor**
Ductwork in ceilings of the top floor,
supply air down

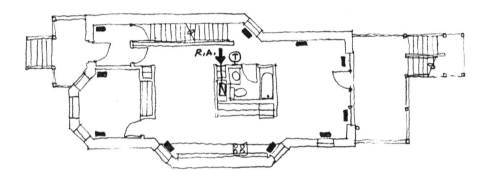

**First Floor**
Supply air grills in floor, central return

While there are multiple systems available to heat and cool a residence, general practice has developed to use a forced air system to supply heated and cooled air with humidification to various areas of a residence.

The central hub of this system is an "air handing unit" (A.H.U.). Simplistically, this is a box with a fan in it, which pushes air past a heating or cooling coil and into a central duct that distributes "supply air" to the perimeters of a house, where heat loss is greatest. The A.H.U., which is typically centrally located in the building, needs "make up air," thus drawing "return air" to it. Thermostats (T) are typically located near the return air (R.A.) grill, and sense the temperature of the returning air, and adjust the temperature and humidity of the home accordingly.

Incorporating ductwork into a Greystone requires design sensitivity, since it requires soffits to run perpendicular to the existing floor framing.

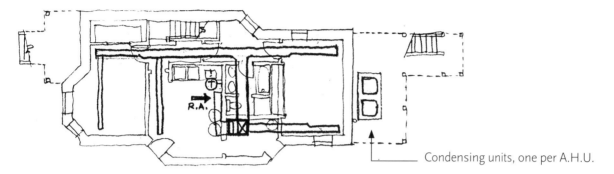

Condensing units, one per A.H.U.

**Basement**
Ductwork in basement ceiling, feed down
and up

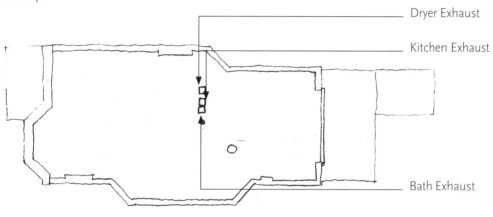

Dryer Exhaust

Kitchen Exhaust

Bath Exhaust

**Roof**

These soffits/dropped ceilings often incorporate other features, such as indirect lighting, to provide additional benefit from this construction.

In addition to air distribution, the mechanical contractor provides exhaust systems for dryers, kitchens and baths. This contractor also installs air conditioning condensers, which provide coolant for heat exchanges at exterior locations.

While at a higher first cost, long term energy savings can be achieved by installing a geo-thermal system, which replaces the condensing units by using the earth's constant temperature as a cooling/heating source.

# Basics of
# Electrical Systems

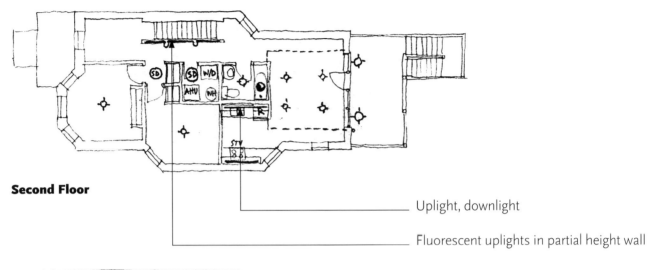

**Second Floor**

Uplight, downlight

Fluorescent uplights in partial height wall

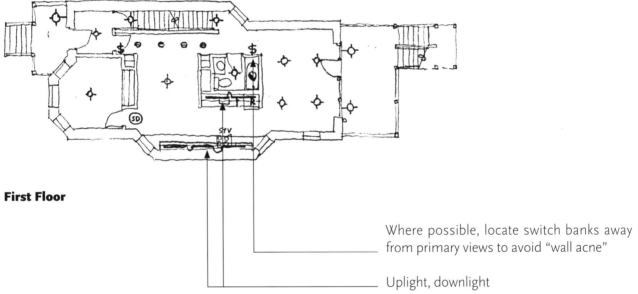

**First Floor**

Where possible, locate switch banks away from primary views to avoid "wall acne"

Uplight, downlight

Electric and telephone services typically arrive to a point on the building from the rear alley either overhead or more recently via underground service. Each dwelling unit is provided an electric meter, and directly inside the unit, an electrical panel with a variety of separate "breakers," small increments of power dedicated to specific tasks/ loads, such as mechanical equipment, lighting, and residential equipment. Depending on the load, many units will be provided with a 100 to 200 Amp service.

The electrician installs smoke (SD) and carbon monoxide (CO) detectors, which local codes will dictate. Power to all equipment, as well as convenience outlets, are dictated by code as well.

The area of greatest design opportunity is developing an energy-efficient lighting system for the residence. Use of fluorescent lamps greatly reduces energy use, and use of indirect lighting of walls and ceilings brightens a space more efficiently than simple down lights.

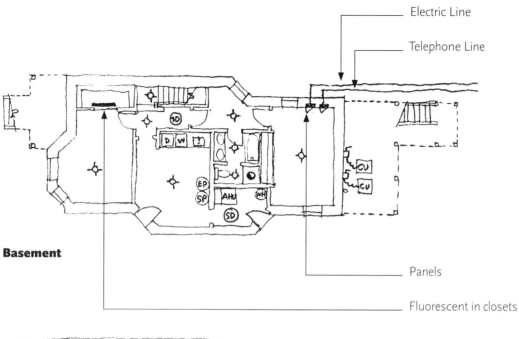

Electric Line

Telephone Line

Panels

Fluorescent in closets

**Basement**

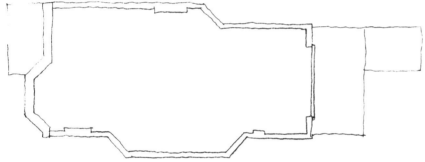

**Roof**

In addition to efficient lamp sources and place-
ments, further economy can be achieved by use
of dimmers to extend lamp life, as well as occupancy sensors to turn off lights when there are no
people in a room. While still at a premium, photovoltaic panels, mounted on the roof will, in time,
provide additional on-site power sources at
affordable prices.

# Basics of
# Plumbing Systems

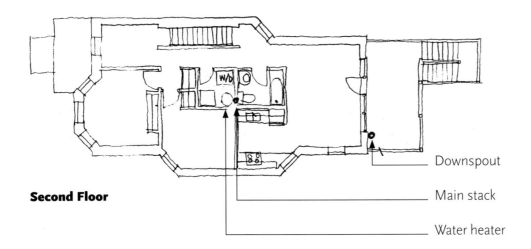

**Second Floor**

Downspout

Main stack

Water heater

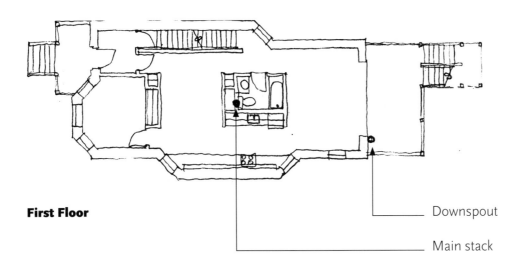

**First Floor**

Downspout

Main stack

Plumbing systems include distribution of water, gas and waste lines throughout a residence. In general, kitchen and bathrooms tend to be clustered together to share access to these distribution systems.

The illustrated plans indicate a central waste (and vent stack) which ideally runs vertically through a residence without major offsets. The bathroom, kitchen and mechanical/laundry areas are grouped around this, thus minimizing piping. Please note that laundry rooms and certain mechanical equipment, such as water heaters and furnaces with air conditioning, require floor drains.

Due to flooding, good practice has developed to include recessed collection pits for waste water and storm water. An ejector pit for waste and a sump pit for storm water collect these fluids and pump them up and overhead, so they can drain by gravity to the sewer. This prevents sewer backups from causing damage to basement improvements.

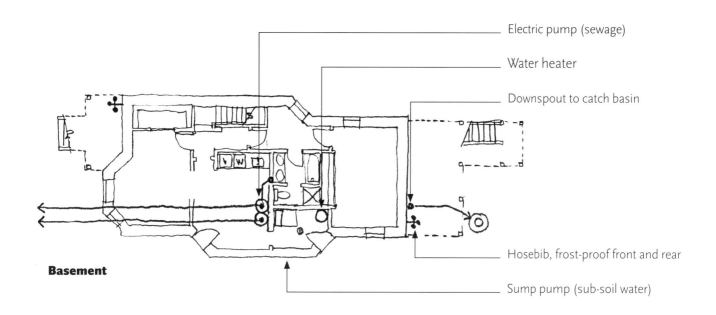

Electric pump (sewage)

Water heater

Downspout to catch basin

Hosebib, frost-proof front and rear

Sump pump (sub-soil water)

**Basement**

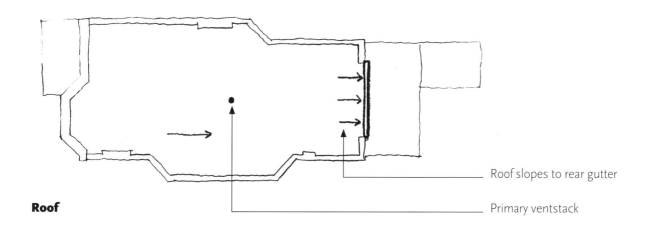

Roof slopes to rear gutter

Primary ventstack

**Roof**

# The Front Yard:

Fitting into the Street, Incrementally

The typical urban Greystone front yard has a responsibility to relate and connect to the larger community of which it is a part. It is enlightening to walk the neighborhood, stopping to photograph and measure the fencing and gates, as well as the height and scale of plantings that seem appropriate and that you admire. Chances are improvements to your Greystone will spur other owners to show their pride of ownership. Individual owners can make their own improvements, but often an informal consensus of revitalization occurs as owners see their confidence in their neighborhood reflected in visible improvements to other properties. Block parties are wonderful opportunities to tour the block and discuss with neighbors the kinds of improvements to common areas, such as sidewalk parkways, which will increase property values for all residents. Such improvements often are organized by the Alderperson and paid for by the city.

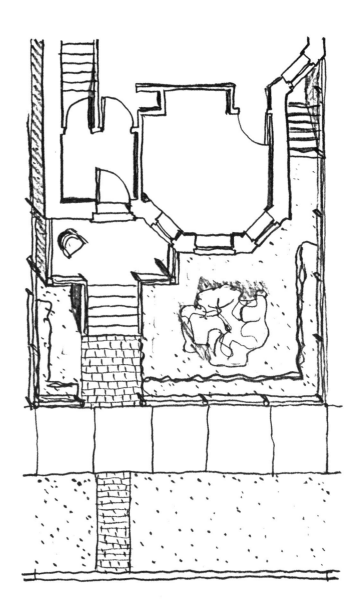

### Step One: Defining Edges

As the saying goes, good fences make good neighbors. The first steps are often defining these edges, by a simple metal rail or fence, or the planting of a border hedge to differentiate the house from the public way. While the path to the front door can be permeable paving, the surrounding yard can be as simple as ground covers planted in decorative gravel. An ornamental tree might be added, planted away from the house.

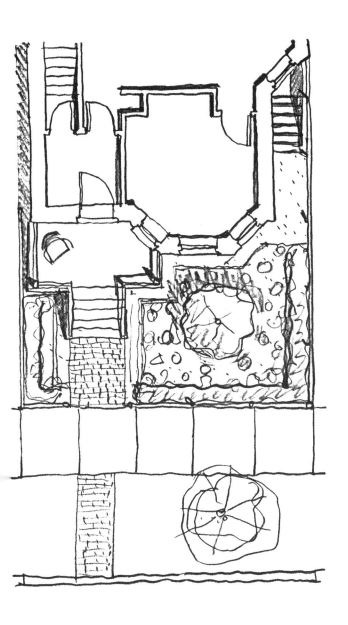

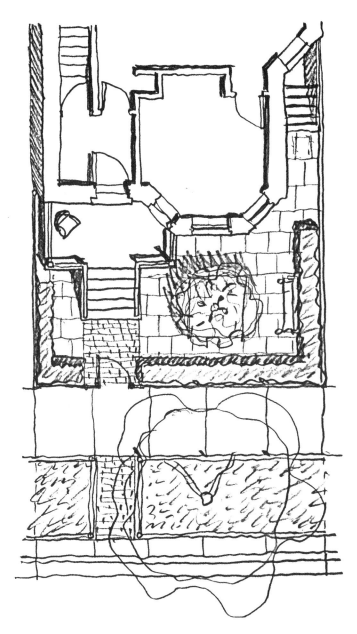

## Step Two: Infill

With the border defined, more articulation of the interior garden, as well as the parkway, is often the next step. Many municipalities will replace parkway trees in poor health, or plant new trees if none exist, helping to shade your yard and front façade. Keeping the perimeter of the house and porch permeable and free from planting is recommended.

## Step Three: Staged Improvements

Depending on the character of the block development, front yards often are further developed with gates, permeable paving for greater use of space by residents, and parkway planting. The latter can be accomplished by using the concept of defining edges with border rails and perimeter plantings to deter pets and pedestrian traffic. The City can and will improve sidewalks and curbs in poor repair. Consult your Alderperson.

# The Rear Yard:

Defining, Using Your Outdoor Room.

The typical urban Greystone backyard has the promise to become the favorite "room" of your house/building. First define its walls and levels of privacy, while maximizing your access to sunlight. Program the "room's" functions: does it need to do one thing, or does it need to do four? Once you determine what and where these things occur, you can begin to determine materials and plants that best support them. These garden rooms are typically smaller than you imagine. Keep them simple in plan first, introducing informality and curves once the basic configuration is in place.

### Step One: Defining Edges
As in the front yard, first define your back yard by fencing and/or with plant material. Define walking zones with gravel or steppers, and identify areas for play and for gardens. Keep it simple.

**Step Two: Infill**

Further define areas of use by paving, edge planting, decorative trees and play equipment as your needs evolve.

**Step Three: Staged Improvements**

Predominant use of permeable paving with localized perimeter planting often maximizes use while still surrounding you with green.

# Additional Information

# Cracking the Codes

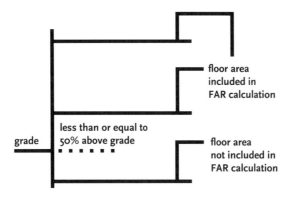

grade

less than or equal to 50% above grade

floor area included in FAR calculation

floor area not included in FAR calculation

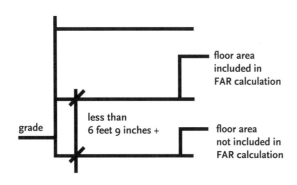

grade

less than 6 feet 9 inches +

floor area included in FAR calculation

floor area not included in FAR calculation

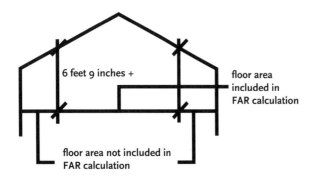

6 feet 9 inches +

floor area included in FAR calculation

floor area not included in FAR calculation

**Zoning Code:**
**How many units, how much area can I add?**

This is a review of the Chicago Zoning and Building Codes. However, it is important to review the current code either on-line or at a library prior to making any changes to your property. This review will focus on a 25 feet x 125 feet piece of property in an RT-4 Residential Zoning District.

*Zoning:* In 1957, the Chicago Zoning Code was adapted to promote public health, safety, welfare and an overall quality of life.

*Zoning Districts:* Chicago is divided into a variety of zoning districts with the intent of maintaining vibrant and attractive residential, commercial, business, and manufacturing districts.

*Residential Districts:* RS — Single Family; RT — 2-flats, townhouses and smaller multi-family buildings; RM — Multi-family buildings.

*Allowed Uses:* See table 17-2-0200 in the code. Generally household, some group living, daycare, etc, are allowable building uses in R zoning districts.

*Lot area:* RT-4 = 1,000 square feet (SF) per dwelling unit. Lot area per unit refers to the amount of lot area required for each dwelling unit on the property. For example, if a minimum lot-area-per-unit standard of 1,000 square feet is applied to 3,125 square foot lot, a maximum of 3 dwelling units would be allowed on the property.

*Floor Area Ratio:* All development in R districts is subject to maximum floor area ratio standard — a ratio of gross floor area to lot size. RT4 districts allow a FAR of 1.2. For example, a 3,125 SF lot x 1.2 would allow 3,750 SF of buildable floor area on the lot. Note that the floor area shall include the area of any floor located below grade or partially below grade when more than one-half of the floor-to-ceiling height of the below-grade (or partially below-grade) unit is above grade level, provided that below-grade or partially below-grade units with a clear height of less than 6 feet 9 inches are not counted as floor area. Additionally any habitable floor area with at least a 6 feet 9 inch ceiling height shall be counted in the floor area.

Yard and Open Space Requirements: RT4 Zoning

*Front Yard:* The greater of 15 feet, 12% of lot depth or an average of the two adjacent lots on either side of the property is required.

*Side Yard:* Both sides combined for 20% of the lot width with a minimum of 2 feet is required. For example, a 25 foot wide lot will require a total of 5 feet with one side being at least 2 feet.

*Rear Yard:* In an RT4 zoning 50 feet or 30% of the lot depth (30% of 125=37.5 feet), whichever is less is required. Parking is allowed in the rear yard.

*Building Height:* In RT4 zones a maximum of 38 feet is allowed. (Be sure to review the building code for number of floors allowed and additional height restrictions.)

*Parking:* 1 parking space per dwelling unit.
Unless otherwise expressly stated, the parking and loading standards apply whenever additional dwelling units are added to an existing residential building or residential use. In such cases, additional off-street parking and loading spaces are required only to serve the additional dwelling units. If the residential building or residential use has been in lawful existence for 50 or more years, the parking and loading standards described apply when 2 or more dwelling units are added.

## Chicago Building Code:
## How and what can I build?

Prior to the Great Chicago Fire, there were no building codes. However in order to have insurance companies insure homeowners, the City needed to institute standards intended to protect the integrity of buildings, as well as the welfare and safety of the public.

The Chicago Department of Construction and Permits requires a building permit for any project that involves structural changes to home or building.

*Types of projects that require permits:*
*Additions* — room, upper floor, expansion
*Attic* — finish, renovate
*Basement* — finish, renovate
*Conversion of units* — single to multiple
*Deck* — build, replace existing deck
*Deconversion of units* — multiple to single dwelling unit
*Demolition* — garage, home, building
*Dormers* — installation
*Electrical system* — alteration, expansion
*Garage* — build attached, detached
*Gut rehab* — complete modernization
*Porch* — build, replace, enclose, renovate

*Habitable Space:* The minimum ceiling height in a habitable room shall not be less than seven feet six inches (with a few exceptions). A basement may be used for habitable rooms if the walls are protected from leakage and dampness and if the required window area is located entirely above the finished elevation of the grade adjoining the wall where the windows are located.

Smoke detectors and carbon monoxide (CO) detectors are required in all single family and multi-family dwelling units.

Access to each apartment unit shall be provided without passing through any part of any other dwelling unit.

Most Greystones are Type III-B, exterior protected masonry buildings. Often the exterior walls are about 12 inch thick and made up of three 4 inch thick widths of brick, with the exterior width being stone (Greystone) on the front and part of the sides.

Type III-B residential buildings may be up to 4 stories and 55 feet in height, except where limited by the zoning. (Note that in a RT4 zoning district the maximum height of a building is limited to 38 feet.)

Additions to type III-B buildings will need to be constructed with masonry or other materials providing 3 hour fire resistance for any bearing wall and 2 hour fire resistance for non bearing walls. Floor construction will require a 1 hour fire resistance.

*Exits:* The primary concern of life safety/code officials, "means of egress" elements such as doors, windows, stairs, are strictly dictated by local codes. Consult the local building code and/or code officials.

In general, in all habitable spaces natural light and ventilation shall be provided. Natural light shall be a minimum of 8% of the floor area and natural ventilation through operable windows shall be a minimum of 4% of the floor area. In kitchens and bathrooms mechanical ventilation of 1.5 CFM per square foot of the room is allowed in lieu of an operable window. Existing buildings may be increased in height and area up to the limits of the building code and zoning code, whichever is more restrictive. When the floor area is increased by not more than 25% of the total floor area of the original building, only the new portion shall conform to all requirements of the code. However when the increase is more than 25% of the total floor area, the entire building shall conform to the code.

Existing porches and decks may be repaired or replaced in the same location with construction of the same type, provided they are designed to meet all load criteria and minimum construction standards identified in the code. If you intend on rebuilding or replacing your porch, please review the Porch and Deck Safety Ordinance before beginning any work.

# Choosing a Contractor

Just as a carpenter learns to "measure twice, cut once," anyone planning any renovation or restoration project should first think through and plan the project well before hiring a contractor or starting the actual work.

Familiarize yourself with the project specifics, *e.g.,* decide what type of materials you want, research material costs, and investigate the permit requirements. There are many publications available that provide guidelines on how long particular types of improvements should take and give general parameters on cost. Larger home improvement stores often have staff available to assist in identifying costs, materials and timelines. Some offer classes on various subjects and have professionals that can answer most of your questions.

## When choosing a contractor you should do the following:

*Get references, including the names and phone numbers of people each contractor has done work for that is similar to the job you want.* Call the references and visit the sites. While a contractor's past performance is not a guarantee for future performance, it is critical that you seek feedback from past customers on how the contractor performed, the level of care shown during the project, whether the schedule was kept, and the timeliness of follow-up on warranty items after the project was completed.

*Ask how long the contractor has been in business and make sure the contractor is licensed to do business in your city/town.* The City of Chicago requires business owners to be licensed, and there are general business and home repair licenses, as well as specific licenses for particular trades, such as plumbing, roofing, electrical, or HVAC. Ask for copies of the licenses the contractor holds.

*Call the Better Business Bureau to ask if there are any complaints on file against the contractor.* In the City of Chicago, you can also check for complaints filed with the Dept. of Consumer Services — call the 311 non-emergency call center to be connected.

*Check that the contractor has proper insurance coverage, which should include Worker's Compensation coverage (this covers any injury workers may incur on the job) and General Liability coverage.* You can ask that the contractor name you as "additional insured" for your project and have the contractor's insurance agent issue an "ACORD" certificate naming you as the "additional insured."

*When soliciting bids for the work to be done, all contractors should bid on the same scope of work so that you can make an informed decision when you compare all of the bids.* Provide contractors with a written list or description of the work that you want to do, so that you receive comparable bids/proposals. If you have particular preferences for materials (*e.g.,* types of cabinets or countertops, plumbing or electrical fixtures, etc.) you should include those preferences in your description of the work to be done. Before they bid, contractors should walk through your home and discuss your project with you. If a contractor suggests an approach or application that differs from what other contractors are bidding on, ask that those different suggestions be specifically itemized and priced in the contractor's bid/proposal.

*All bids for work to be performed should be in writing and be specific enough so that you can see what each item costs (a "line-item" bid).* For the best comparison, ask for line-item bids from at least three contractors. Contractors should provide you with a free estimate for the work in the form of a written bid/proposal; you should not have to pay to get a bid/proposal from a contractor. Many contractors use an actual contract form for their bid/proposal, so you should be careful not to sign the estimate/bid/proposal because doing so may obligate you and create a contractual relationship. Do not use contractors who will not give a firm bid. If a contractor says that a firm bid cannot be provided because of problems that might be found once the work actually begins, you should find another contractor to bid on your project.

*Agree on the payment.* The contractor's bid/proposal may be broken out by line items (so that you can make comparisons), but when you sign the contract it will be for the full amount. Once the contract is signed you will not have the right to negotiate individual line item costs. Contracts can be either for "time and materials" or a contracted amount. The full cost of a "time and materials" contract is difficult to predict because you will be paying an hourly rate for the contractor's time as well as the cost of materials. For your own budgeting and planning, it generally is better to enter into a contract that has a stipulated price for the entire project. Be aware that most projects will ultimately include changes in the scope and cost of work — because of things that are added or taken away from the original proposal. You should plan on having at least 10% more than the contract price available for these contingencies and Change Orders.

*While most contractors will ask for a significant portion of the contract price before the work begins, it is a common practice to make partial payments to the contractor as work is completed.* You can write into the contract that you will pay a certain percentage of the cost when a certain percentage of the work is done, or you can specify a payment schedule based on completing various line items in the proposal. It is advisable that you do not give the contractor any money before the work is started. In some cases, if you have hired a contractor who has a smaller operation and if your project includes items that need to be fabricated to fit your home (such as new windows), the contractor may not have the capital to pay the deposit to the manufacturer. In such cases, if you choose to advance money for the windows or for any other materials, you should do so only directly to the supplier or manufacturer and based on an invoice. If you are beginning a large project and the contractor either does not have credit with suppliers or cannot afford to buy supplies and equipment, you would do well to use a different contractor.

*Specify responsibility for permits and licenses.* If the work on your house requires building permits or inspections, your contractor should apply for the permits before the work begins and make arrangements for the inspections as the work progresses. The cost of permits should be included in the bid/proposal price. The contractor should also have the appropriate license for the job. If a contractor is charging for obtaining a license, then you should think twice about using a contractor who does not have the appropriate license to begin the work.

*Do not sign an estimate/bid/proposal unless it is with the contractor you have selected.* Even then, you should sign the contract only when the bid/proposal states exactly what work is to be done, when and how payments will be made, and everything else you have agreed upon. The contract should specify dates for when the work will begin and an estimated date on which the work will be completed. The contract should say exactly how you will know whether work is done properly and what will happen if the work is not completed on schedule.

*Ask about the warranty or guarantee the contractor will give.* It is standard practice for the contractor to warranty the work for at least one year — covering the materials installed and the contractor's work. Certain elements will have longer manufacturers' warranties (such as roofing material, heating units, etc.) and the contractor should provide you with all of the written warranties for all of these items. All warranties and guarantees should be in writing.

*Do not let the contractor make any changes to the contract unless you have approved it in writing.* Any changes to the contract will have an impact on the cost of the project — either increases or decreases. Be sure that you have the funds to pay for any increases before you agree to them, or else you may be subject to a lawsuit if you cannot pay for the changes when the time comes.

*Do not make the final payment until the work is finished.* Include in your contract what amount will be withheld as the final payment. You can also specify that you will hold back up to 10 percent of the total cost until the final inspections are completed by the building inspector or a third party that you hire to inspect the work (such as an architect or construction manager).

A large project may require architectural drawings in order for permits to be issued. Architects can also be hired to represent an owner throughout the project, conducting inspections and verifying that work has been done according to a plan. If you obtain a "construction" or home improvement loan for the work, your lender may have an inspector who will verify that work is in place before payments are made to a contractor, but do not consider this a substitute for your own inspection and satisfaction with the work. If you obtain a Home Equity loan to pay for the work, the lender will provide you access to the loan proceeds for whatever purpose you wish and will not make any inspections of the work. Some non-profit organizations offer technical assistance to home owners doing these kinds of repairs. Around the country, the NeighborWorks network of non-profit organizations (including NHS of Chicago) offer a range of technical assistance in conjunction with loans for home improvement.

# Recommended Specifications
# for a Green Building

## Mechanical Specifications

*Boiler*
· sealed combustion/direct vent 88% AFUE

*Furnace*
· sealed combustions/direct vent,
  minimum 90% AFUE
· ≥ 50% total heat load

*Air Conditioning*
· minimum SEER of 14

*Water Heater*
· sealed combustion/direct vent ≥ 60% EF
· sealed combustion/direct vent 88% for
  central system

*Ventilation/Forced Air System*
· ≥ 75 CFM at .25 static pressure exhaust
  fans for bathrooms
· ≥ 150 CFM exhaust fan in kitchen

*Lighting*
· compact fluorescent motion sensor fixtures
  for exterior lighting
· compact fluorescent bulbs used for
  interior lighting

*Combined HVAC*
· adopt a commissioning plan to verify and
  ensure that the HVAC system is designed,
  installed and operated as intended to ensure
  maximum efficiency

*Thermostat*
· Energy Star® rated programmable model

*Plumbing*
· aerator restricting flow faucets

## Building Materials

*Windows*
· Low-E coating, argon gas insulated
· maximum U-Value of .35 or R-Value of 2.88

*Insulation*
Recycled content material (cellulose,
soy based, denim based)
R-Values:
· sidewalls ≥ R19 (full cavity blown insulation
  if possible)
· attic of ≥ R43
· ducts sealed with duct mastic or
  approved tape
· hot/cold pipes 3 feet from water heater
· basement
  ≥ R19 full ceiling insulation over
  unconditioned basement
  ≥ R10 in basement band joist if basement
  unconditioned

*Roofing*
75% of the entire roof area should have
high solar reflectance:
· emissivity of at least 0.9
· initial solar reflectance of .65
· 3 year solar reflectance of .50

*Lumber*
· 3rd party certified sustainably
  harvested sources

## Finishes

*Paints*
· Low or No VOC content paints and finishes
· water-based urethane floor finishes
· low toxicity adhesives and sealants

*Cabinets*
- reclaimed, re-milled or sustainably harvested woods
- 0% formaldehyde particle board

*Floors*
- domestic wood flooring from reused, recovered or re-milled sources
- sustainably harvested bamboo
- sustainably harvested cork
- natural fiber carpet

*Appliances*
- Energy Star® rated

*Landscaping*
- use native plants
- reduce lawn size
- compost vegetation
- mow with reel mower

## Additional Environmental Upgrades

*Rain barrels*
- use captured rain or recycled site water to reduce potable water consumption for irrigation (capture roof water from downspouts into rain barrel containers)

*Active Solar Heating*
- Solar Fraction ≥ 20%
- www.solar-rating.org

*Solar Domestic Hot Water System*
- ≥ 50% of annual hot water needs
- www.solar-rating.org

*Tankless Water Heater*
- direct vent, power vented gas-fired, or electric tankless water heater
- www.gamanet.org

*Solar Electric System*
- photovoltaic panels to help meet the electric load of the home
- www.exceloncorp.com

*Blower Door Testing*
- not to exceed .25 CFM/50SF of building envelope area

## Landscaping
- restore a minimum of 50% of the site area (excluding the building footprint) by replacing impervious surfaces with native or adapted vegetation.

## Waste Disposal
- establish a Construction and Demolition recycling plan
- dispose of hazardous materials property (*i.e.* lead and asbestos)
- re-use original material whenever possible

# Glossary

**Air Valve** A device for regulating the flow of air through a pipe system.

**Anodized Aluminum** Aluminum that has been coated with a film of aluminum oxide through an electrolytic process. This film protects the aluminum and serves as a paint base.

**Apron** Horizontal trim board under a window stool.

**Backsaw** A saw that has a reinforcing metal strip along its back edge.

**Baluster** One of a series of short posts supporting a rail or coping (q.v.), as along the edge of a staircase.

**Balustrade** Unit of a staircase consisting of the handrail and the vertical posts and newel posts supporting it, as along the edge of a staircase.

**Baseboard** A finishing board that covers a plastered wall at its base where it meets the floor.

**Batt Insulation** Insulating material, usually composed of mineral fibers, made in small units for ease of installation between studs or joists.

**Bay Window** A projection from a building, beginning on the ground floor and sometimes rising several stories, filled by one or more windows at each story.

**Beadboard** Decorative wood paneling, with rounded "bead" profile between boards.

**Beadboard Ceiling** A tongue and groove paneling incorporating one or more half-round beads milled into the finished surface. It is often used for wainscoting, and as a finish for porch ceilings.

**Beam** Horizontal structural member of long span that supports the floors of a building.

**Belt Course** A horizontal section or strip of wood, stone, or brick applied at the same level across or all around a building.

**Beveled Glass** Glass with a sloping edge where the angle between two sides is either greater or less than a right angle.

**Board and Batten** A type of exterior siding made up of wide boards overlaid with narrow strips at the joints. Vertical board and batten siding is often found in Gothic Revival buildings (1830–1860) while its horizontal counterpart can be seen in Prairie School architecture (1900–1920).

**Bracket** An L-shaped device, one arm of which is anchored to a vertical support, with the other arm extending horizontally to support a projecting balcony or shelf.

**Butt Hinge** A hinge with one leaf attached to the edge of a door and the other to door jamb.

**Butt Joint** A joint formed when two surfaces are put together end-to-end or edge-to-edge.

**Cap** The top of a column (abbreviation for capital).

**Capillary Action** Force that results when the adhesion of a liquid to a solid is great than the internal cohesion of the liquid itself, causing the liquid to be raised against a vertical surface.

**Casement Window** A window hinged on one of its vertical edges to that it can open inward or outward, as a door opens.

**Casing** The framing around window or a door.

**Cast Iron** Pipes, railing, or other metal objects formed by pouring molten iron into a mold.

**Catch Basin** A receptacle for catching water runoff from a designated area; usually a shallow concrete box with a grating and a discharge pipe leading to a plumbing or stormwater system.

**Cementitious Parging** A thin cement-based coat applied to concrete to fill and level the surface.

**Chair Rail** A wooden molding around the wall of a room at chair-back height. Originally meant to protect the wall from damage; often installed as an ornamental feature.

**Chalking** The effect of weather on exterior paint; the process breaks up particles of the paint surface, leaving a chalk-like residue.

**Checking** Cracks that appear in the upper layers of exterior paint coatings which may eventually penetrate the entire coating.

**Circuit** The path of electrical current from one point to another.

**Circuit Breaker** A switch that automatically breaks the flow of electrical current to a circuit when that circuit is overloaded.

**Civil Engineer** A professional trained in the design and construction of public works.

**Clapboard** A long, narrow board, with the bottom edge thicker than the top, that is used horizontally, each board overlapping the one below it, as siding on a building.

**Condensing unit** A cooling system's outdoor component, which includes a compressor and condensing coil designed to discharge heat.

**Coping** A covering at the top of brick or stone walls that prevents water from seeping along side of the wall.

**Cornice** A horizontal, molded ornamental projection along the top of a building that usually finishes and caps a structure.

**Course** One horizontal row of rocks or stones.

**Crawl Space** The shallow space between the surface of the ground and the first floor.

**Cupola** A small decorative dome or tower attached to and rising above the roof of a building.

**Damper** In a fireplace system, the metal vent or device located at the top of the firebox *(q.v.)* which can be opened to regulate the draft of the flue above.

**Decking** Pieces set in place to form a finished surface on which one may walk.

**Dentil** One of a series of small rectangular or square blocks arranged in a band, like a row of teeth projecting from the lower part of a cornice or molding.

**Detached House** An individual structure with all exterior sides exposed.

**Dormer Window** A vertical window set against a sloping roof with its own small roof and supporting walls; used to add space, light, and air to attic rooms.

**Double-Hung Window** A window with two vertically moving sashes, each closing a different part of the window. *Note:* A single-hung window is visually identical, with the upper sash fixed.

**Downspout** The pipe that carries water from roof gutters *(q.v.)* to the ground.

**Drain-tile** A perforated, corrugated plastic pipe laid at the bottom of the foundation wall and used to drain excess water away from the foundation. It prevents ground water from seeping through the foundation wall. Sometimes called perimeter drain.

**Drainage Mat** A prefabricated drainage system, in sheet form, installed under and around foundations and slabs to aid in the drainage of water away from a structure.

**Drip Cap** An exterior wood or masonry molding that directs water off of and away from a structure. Usually used at the top of door and window frames, and where wall sheathing and foundation meet.

**Dry Wall** Prefabricated panels, consisting of gypsum plaster lined with paper, that can be nailed directly onto wall studs or over existing plaster walls. Also called sheetrock, gypsum board, or plasterboard.

**Dumpster** A large refuse container that can be emptied into a garbage truck.

**Duplex** A house divided into two living units with a separate entrance for each.

**DWV** Commonly used abbreviation for the piping which forms the drain, waste, and vent portion of a plumbing system.

**Eaves** The part of the roof that projects horizontally beyond the side walls of a building.

**Efflorescence** The white powdery substance that forms on the outer surface of masonry wall, due to the evaporation of water from chemical compounds in the masonry.

**Ejector pit** A sealed chamber for storing sewage and periodically pumping it up to a sewer at a higher level.

**Electric Pump** A pump powered by electric current.

**ERV: Energy Recovery Ventilation** A system of using available excess heat energy to reheat/preheat incoming air or water.

**Etched Glass** Clear or mirrored glass on which decorative designs have been produced by strong acid corroding selected areas of the surface.

**Extruded Metal** Metal that has been forced or pressed out into a shaped piece.

**Façade** The face of a building; in particular, the elevation which has been given special architectural treatment.

**Face-nailing** To nail into the surface face of a piece of wood.

**Faceplate** Metal plate covering the surface of a door immediately behind the door knob.

**Feathering-In** The process of toothing in materials such as brick or stone into similar adjacent surfaces to visually and structurally tie new infill to old.

**Finish Coat** The final coat of plaster which gives a wall or ceiling a smooth surface.

**Finish Floor** The topmost layer of wood, tile, or other decorative flooring material that is applied over the rougher subfloor.

**Firebox** That part of a fireplace in which the fuel is actually burned.

**Fish Wire** Electrical wiring to which new wiring is attached and by which means the new wires can be drawn through enclosed walls; also called fish tape.

**Flashing** Thin sheet-metal strips applied to joints or angles of a building to prevent water leakage.

**Flue** The vertical shaft, usually lined with metal or tile, of a chimney or pipe that directs smoke, gases, or air out of a building.

**Flush Door** A flat, unpaneled door that may be of solid core (no space between front and back sides) or hollow core (has space between front and back) construction.

**Foamed Polyurethane** see Polyurethane.

**Footing** The widened base of a foundation, which distributes the building weight over a greater surface area.

**Foundation** A building's sub-structure, typically below grade, that carries the weight of the building down to the ground.

**Framing** The wooden or metal skeleton of a partition wall or building.

**Gable** The triangular upper portion of a wall at the end of a pitched roof.

**Galvanic Action** The rust-producing effect of contact between two dissimilar metals.

**General Contractor** In a construction project, a person who agrees to supply materials, services, and/or supervision for a certain price, and may arrange with subcontractors *(q.v.)* for supplying specific materials or services.

**Girder** A large horizontal beam of wood or steel that supports walls or joists *(q.v.)*.

**Glazing** The action of putting glass in windows or doors.

**Gutter** A trough, usually of metal, placed along the eaves of a roof to catch water and direct it to the downspout *(q.v.)*.

**Gypsum Board** see Drywall.

**Hardwood** Wood from broad-leaved trees, such as oak, maple, and poplar.

**Header** A brick or stone laid with its short side parallel to the wall plane.

**Hearth** The floor of the fireplace or the floor immediately in front of the fireplace.

**Hose Bib** An exterior water faucet.

**HVAC** Abbreviation for Heating, Ventilation, and Air Conditioning.

**Jamb** The vertical pieces in a window or door frame.

**Joint** In masonry, the mortar between two bricks or pieces of stone.

**Joist** A horizontal beam laid parallel with other beams to support a floor or ceiling.

**Lath** Strips of wood (in older houses) or metal mesh (in newer houses) that are attached to supporting elements in the wall frame and to which plaster is applied.

**Lattice panel** Pre-fabricated sheets of criss-crossed wood or plastic lath (thin strips) that is frequently used for trellises or semi-private fencing.

**Leaded Glass** Small pieces of glass held together by lead or zinc bars to fill a window frame.

**Lintel** A wood, stone, or steel beam above a window or door opening that supports the weight of that part of the wall immediately above the opening; a round-headed lintel is rounded and a flat-headed one is horizontal.

**Load-bearing Wall** A wall that actually supports the weight of a building.

**Lug Sill** A window sill built into the wall which runs horizontally beyond the masonry opening.

**Main Stack** The three sections — the soil stack, waste stack, and vent stack — of the vertical pipes that comprise a plumbing waste system. A soil stack carries waste disposal from water closets. A waste stack carries waste disposal from all other fixtures. A vent stack provides air circulation throughout the waste system and allows for the release of sewer gases.

**Mantel** The decorative material that surrounds a fireplace, including the shelf attached to the chimney just above the fireplace.

**Masonry** Anything made of brick, stone, cement, concrete, or tile.

**Medallion** A plaster ornament found in the middle of ceilings in late nineteenth-century homes, and from which a light fixture was hung.

**Molding** Strips of wood or metal, plain or embellished with patterns, used for ornamental or finishing purposes.

**Mortise and Tenon** A method of joining two pieces of wood in which one piece has a projection that fits into a corresponding hole in the other piece.

**Nail Set** A pointed tool used in conjunction with a hammer to drive a nail farther into a surface than the hammer alone permits.

**Parapet** A low wall along the edge of a roof.

**Parging** See Cementitous Parging.

**Parquet Floor** A floor made of pieces of wood, often of contrasting colors and varying shapes, laid in a decorative pattern.

**Parting Strip** A strip of wood that separates the upper and lower sash of a double-hung window (q.v.).

**Pediment** A decorative form, usually triangular, atop a structure, especially over a portico; derived from triangular members in classical architecture that topped the front of a structure.

**Pentachlorophenol (penta)** A chemical wood preservative.

**Permeable paving** Road, parking lot, and walkway paving that allows water and air to move through the paving material.

**Photovoltaic panels** A panel that collects and converts solar energy into electricity or heat.

**Pier** Vertical columnar supports of a wall.

**Pigment** A coloring agent which is mixed with water or oil to make paint.

**Pilaster** A rectangular column with a base, shaft, and capital that is attached to a wall. It can serve structural needs by reinforcing a wall, or it can be applied for merely decorative purposes.

**Pilot Hole** A hole made in wood, by means of a drill or nail, to direct a screw.

**Pipe Chase** A duct or groove cut in a floor or wall to hold or conceal pipes.

**Plaster** A soft mixture of lime with sand or cement and water for spreading on walls and ceilings to form a hard finish surface when dried.

**Plasterboard** see Drywall

**Plastic Wood** A plastic material, usually in paste form, used to fill cracks or holes in wood.

**Plate Rail** A narrow molding attached to the dining room wall, about ¾ of the way up the wall, used to hold decorative china plates.

**Plinth Block** A base molding at the intersection of the baseboard and the door casing.

**Plumbing Stack** see Main Stack.

**Polyurethane Resin** used in chemical-resistant coatings, adhesives, and electrical insulation; when in spray form, it is called foamed polyurethane.

**Portland Cement** An extremely strong cement composed of limestone and clay and resembling Portland stone, a limestone quarried at Portland, England.

**Post** An upright support.

**Posthole footing** A simple footing for a post for a porch or deck, generally 8 to 12 inches wide and extending below the frost line, formed by digging a vertical post-hole and filling it with concrete.

**Poultice** A soft, dense mixture of various substances spread on a cloth or similar material and applied to a surface to clean it or draw out stains.

**Pressure Wash** A method of cleaning a surface with a liquid cleaning agent applied under pressure.

**Primer** First coat of paint or similar substance applied to a surface.

**Rafter** A roof member, often sloping, that supports the roof covering and extends from the eaves to the ridge (q.v.) of the roof.

**Railing** A barrier or guard that consists of a rail supported by vertical posts.

**Ranch Molding** A style of molding devoid of ornamentation that is narrow at the top and wide at the base with a curved profile.

**Rehabilitation** The process of returning a property to a state of utility, through repair or alteration, making possible an efficient contemporary use. Important historical or architectural features are preserved or restored.

**Remodeling** The process of making over a house or part of a house, so its original distinguishing features and overall character are often changed.

**Renovation** The process of repairing certain aspects of a house by replacing worn or broken parts with brand new parts, for example electrical circuitry, heating plant, and the like.

**Resilient Channel** A metal furring member designed to absorb sound or noise impact that strikes the surfacing membrane.

**Restoration** The process of restoring existing construction, maintaining original materials and returning the finishes and fittings to the original condition.

**Reveal** The vertical face of a window opening.

**Ridge** In a pitched roof, the horizontal line created at the top of the sloping roof planes.

**Riser** The vertical part of a step.

**Rosette** An ornament with parts arranged in a circular pattern much like a rose.

**Row House** A house connected to other houses by common walls to form a continuous group or row.

**Running Molding** Ornamental molding with a wave-like pattern used in a frieze or band.

**Rusticated** Finished with a rough masonry surface.

**Saddle Threshold** A strip of wood or metal beveled on each edge and used above the finished floor under outside doors.

**Sandblasting** A method of cleaning brick or stone whereby sand is propelled at high velocity by a blast of steam or air creating an abrasive action that wears away the outer surface of the masonry; the process can expose the brick or stone to deterioration. Should NOT be used on Chicago Greystone.

**Sash** The outer frame around the glass in a window.

**Scratch Coat** The first and roughest coat of a three layer plaster finish; followed by the smoother brown coat and finished by the finish coat.

**Service Box** A metal box that houses a building's main electrical switch and its fuses.

**Sheetrock** see Drywall

**Sill** The horizontal element beneath a window or door opening.

**Single Pane Window** A window with one pane of glass separating the interior from the exterior.

**Smoke Chamber** The area above the smoke shelf and below the flue *(q.v.)* of a fireplace.

**Smoke Shelf** A projection at the base of the smoke chamber in a fireplace that prevents downward air currents from forcing smoke into the room.

**Soffit** The underside of an arch, eave, beam or stairway.

**Sola-Tubes**® A tubular skylight that captures and redirects sunlight down a reflective shaft into an interior space.

**Spandrel** The wall area between the head of a window on one story and the sill of a window on the floor above.

**Splash Board** An element around a sink or tub that protects the wall from splashed water.

**Stained Glass** Glass colored throughout by metallic oxides or into whose surface pigments have been burned; used for decorative purposes, especially for windows.

**Steam Cleaning** Cleaning a masonry surface by steam applied under pressure.

**Steam Valve** A valve that regulates a supply of steam, as in a radiator.

**Stool** The wooden shelf-like element inside and extending across the base of a window opening.

**Storm Window** An extra window usually placed on the outside of an existing window as additional protection against cold weather and air infiltration.

**Stretcher** A brick or stone laid with its long side parallel to the wall plane.

**Stringcourse** A continuous, sometimes molded, horizontal band on an exterior wall, usually decorative in nature.

**Structural Walls** Walls that support any vertical loads of a building in addition to their own weight.

**Stud** An upright post in the framing of a wall to which lath, wallboard, sheathing, or paneling is applied or fastened.

**Subcontractor** An individual or firm that enters into a contract to perform part or all of another's contract to provide goods or services.

**Subfloor** The rough boards that rest directly on the joists and serve as a floor during construction. After construction is completed the finish floor is laid over the subfloor.

**Sump pit** A sump is a specially made receiving tank to receive wastes or sewage by gravity; from the sump the wastes or sewage is lifted by pump or ejectors to be discharged into the building drain or building sewer.

**Sump Pump** A small capacity pump that empties pits receiving groundwater, sewage, or liquid waste.

**Surround** Something that enframes a central object.

**Terne-metal** Sheet iron or steel coated with an alloy of lead and tin.

**Terra-Cotta** Hard-baked clay often used for ornamentation on the exterior of buildings, as well as tile copings.

**Thermal Capacity** The ability of a given material to accept heat.

**Thermopaned** A window with two layers of glass separated by an air space in order to protect against heat gain or loss.

**Three-flat** A three-story building in which each story contains a one-story residential unit

**Throat** The part of a chimney above the fireplace where the walls of the flue *(q.v.)* converge as a means of increasing the updraft.

**Tooth** The roughness on an undercoat of paint that enables it to grip the finish coat.

**Topcoat** A final coating, as of paint.

**Tongue and groove decking** Lumber, having a projecting edge and a grooved mating edge, placed over roof or floor structural members for structural rigidity of building frame and to provide a surface for traffic or substrate for roofing or flooring system.

**Transom Window** A small window, frequently hinged, above a door or another window.

**Tread** The horizontal part of a stair.

**Tuck-point** Repair of defective, mortar joints in brick masonry, due to cracking, crumbling, or erosion.

**Turret** A small tower-shaped projection of a building.

**Two-flat** A two-story building in which each story contains a one-story residential unit.

**Union Nut** Radiator nut between the steam valve and the radiator fins.

**Valley** The place where two distinct slopes of a roof meet.

**Vapor Barrier** Material used in walls to prevent moisture and thus prevent condensation within a wall.

**Varnish Stain** A varnish with pigment added for coloration.

**Veneer** A thin layer of finished material, such as wood, applied over a substratum of material of lesser quality or grade.

**Vent Pipe** A pipe that admits air to the interior of a structure for ventilation; also a small pipe that connects a plumbing fixture to the main vent stack.

**Venting Stacks/Vent Stack** Piping in a plumbing waste system that provides air circulation throughout the system and allows for the release of sewer gases.

**Vents** Openings that permit the movement of air in and out of a building.

**Vestibule** A small room at the entrance way of a building.

**VOC paint** Paint containing Volatile Organic Compounds. These compounds release low level toxic emissions into the air.

**Wainscoting** Another term for wood paneling; it is also used in regard to paneling that goes up to chair-rail height.

**Wallboard** Large rigid sheets of boarding made from a variety of materials and used for sheathing interior walls and ceilings.

**Water Table** The level below which the ground is saturated with water.

**Weight Box** A concealed wooden vertical "box" into which iron counterweights and chains would reside, balancing the movement of traditional double-hung wood window sash. This box typically sits within a widened masonry opening just inside of the exterior wythe of masonry.

**Wood Lath** Flat strip of wood used to form a foundation for plaster on ceilings and walls.

*Source*
*Many of these glossary entries are from City House: A Guide to Renovating Older Chicago-Area Houses (Commission on Chicago Historical and Architectural Landmarks, 1979).*

# Resources

**Home Repair/Rehab Grants, Loans, Technical Assistance**
Historic Chicago Greystone Initiative®
Neighborhood Housing Services of Chicago
3555 West Ogden Avenue
Chicago, IL 60623
773.522.4637
773.522.4890 *f*
www.nhschicago.org

Neighborhood Housing Services of Chicago
(Central Office)
1279 N. Milwaukee Avenue, 5th Floor
Chicago, IL 60622
773.329.4010
773.329.4120 *f*
www.nhschicago.org

Emergency Housing Assistance Program
(EHAP)
City of Chicago
Department of Housing
311
www.cityofchicago.org/housing

**Street and Community**
Tree Planting on Public Ways
311

Dead or Damaged Trees, Dead Animals,
Debris Removal, Graffiti, Vandalism
311

Sidewalks, Streets, Alleys and Cul-de-Sac Repairs
311

**Energy Efficiency and Green Building**
Residential Energy Assessment Program (REAP)
City of Chicago
Department of Environment
http://webapps.cityofchicago.org/ERC/

CEDA Home Weatherization Program
City of Chicago
Department of Housing
1.800.571.CEDA
www.cityofchicago.org/housing

Green Permit Program
City of Chicago
Department of Construction and Permits
www.cityofchicago.org/dcap

Green Homes Program
City of Chicago
Department of Environment
www.cityofchicago.org/environment

Lead-Safe Homes Initiative
City of Chicago
Department of Public Health
312.747.LEAD (5323)

Chicago Center for Green Technology (CCGT)
City of Chicago
Department of Environment
312.746.9642
www.cityofchicago.org/environment/GreenTech

Low Income Home Energy Assistance Program
1.800.571.2332
http://www.liheapillinois.com/community.html

Illinois Home Weatherization Assistance
Program (IHWAP)
http://www.weatherizationillinois.com/

U. S. Green Building Council
Leadership in Energy and Environmental Design
(LEED)
www.usgbc.org

U. S. Green Building Council
Chicago Chapter
312.746.4679
www.usgbc-chicago.org

U.S. Green Building Council (LEED for Homes)
www.usgbc.org/leed/homes/

Energy Star®
U.S. Department of Energy
www.energystar.gov/

Energy Efficiency and Renewable Energy
U.S. Department of Energy
www.eere.energy.gov/

National Fenestration Rating Council
www.nfrc.org

Efficient Windows Collaborative
www.efficientwindows.org

## Accessibility and Independent Living

Home Repairs for Accessible and Independent
Living (H-RAIL)
City of Chicago
Department of Housing
www.cityofchicago.org/housing

Housing Information Services
The Mayor's Office for People with Disabilities
(MOPD) Housing Program
312.744.6673
www.cityofchicago.org/mayor

## Landscaping

The Chicago Botanic Garden
847.835.5440
www.chicagobotanic.org

City Wide Plant Distribution Days
Greencorps Chicago
312.744.8691
www.cityofchicago.org/environment

Free Seeds
America the Beautiful Fund
1.800.522.3557
http://www.america-the-beautiful.org/
free_seeds/

## Historic Preservation

National Trust for Historic Preservation
(Midwest Office)
312.939.5547
www.nationaltrust.org/midwest/

Landmarks Preservation Council of Illinois
312.922.1742
www.landmarks.org

City of Chicago
Landmarks Division
312.744.3200
www.cityofchicago.org/Landmarks

National Park Services
Technical Preservation Services
http://www.nps.gov/history/hps/tps/index.htm

Secretary of the Interior's Standards for the
Treatment of Historic Properties
www.nps.gov/history/hps/tps/standards_
guidelines.htm

## Architectural Services

American Institute of Architects
www.aia.org

American Institute of Architects
Chicago Chapter
312.670.7770
www.aiachicago.org

National Organization of Minority Architects
(NOMA)
www.noma.net

Chicago Architecture Foundation
312.922.3432
www.architecture.org

*Note:* The City of Chicago
has implemented the 311
system as a "one-stop
shopping" center for
access to all city services
and non-emergency po-
lice services. Chicago
residents can now call 311
— 24 hours a day, 7 days a
week — to report service
needs, check the status of
previous service requests,
obtain information
regarding City programs
or events and file police
reports. Service requests
can also be entered
online at http://
www.cityofchicago.org

# Contributors/Advisors

## Contributors

*David Brown*
City Design Center and
School of Architecture
University of Illinois at Chicago
Glossary and Resources

*Robert Bruegmann*
Department of Art History
University of Illinois at Chicago
The Greystone: No Ordinary Building

*Matt Cole*
Neighborhood Housing Services of Chicago
Choosing a Contractor

*Tasneem A. Chowdhury*
School of Architecture
University of Illinois at Chicago
Co-Editor
Glossary and Resources

*Roberta M. Feldman*
City Design Center
School of Architecture
University of Illinois at Chicago
Moving the Walls

*Rachel Forman*
Chicago Associates Planners and Architects
Preserving the Stone

*Thomas Forman*
School of Architecture
University of Illinois at Chicago
Chicago Associates Planners and Architects
Preserving the Stone

*Matthew Gaynor*
School of Art and Design
University of Illinois at Chicago
Art Direction

*Corinna Gelster*
School of Art and Design
University of Illinois at Chicago
Graphic Design

*Peter Landon*
City Design Center and
School of Architecture
University of Illinois at Chicago
Landon Bone Baker Architects
Focus Front Façade
Focus Rear Façade
Cracking the Codes

*Charles Leeks*
Neighborhood Housing Services of Chicago
General Overview
Preface

*Seth Reimer*
Department of Environment
City of Chicago
Environmental Recommendations
Recommended Specifications for a
Green Building

*Darris Shaw*
Neighborhood Housing Services of Chicago
Choosing a Contractor

*James Wheaton*
Neighborhood Housing Services of Chicago
Co-Editor

*Dan Wheeler*
School of Architecture
University of Illinois at Chicago
Wheeler Kearns Architects
Co-Editor and Primary Illustrator